NEOMONISM

NEOMONISM

DINO MEURS

To order additional copies of this book, contact:
Xlibris Corporation
1-888-795-4274
www.Xlibris.com
Orders@Xlibris.com
65405

Contents

Introramble

What follows this introramble are *re*presentations of various conversations I've been in over the years concerning my particular views of Spiritual matters as an unschooled mystic. This book started out as templates for lectures as I once considered becoming a philosophy professor in college. Due to a couple reasons, I had to leave college and put aside the writing for a while. When I got back to them a few years later, the lectures did not have the same appeal; they sounded like I was telling people how to believe. I would rather discuss what I believe and why I belief it so I did my best to turn lectures into conversations. Some of these conversations are closely related to others, but the resemblance is like the viewing of a mountain from different locations. Just as one can pinpoint a target through triangulation, one can discuss theology from many angles for no one angle, in and of itself, is Absolute Truth.

People have asked me about my spelling of the Holy Name. When I use the '-O-'spelling, you can insert the pronunciation "God". The way I spell it is just a visual *re*presentation of my nonimage of the Divine and not to be taken as the name of "another God", as some have claimed. I have a lot of respect for the Jewish tradition of not spelling out the Holy Title but I cannot follow their spelling as I have a different -O-image than what they have and for the same reason, I cannot spell it 'Brahma' nor 'Allah.' Rather than coming up with a different Title, I came up with a different spelling. I have never been fond of 'the Name is the Thing' type of thinking that gets carried to the extreme of some people acting as if the word "Whiskey" will get them drunk.

When this type of stuff happens, and it happens in all schools of thought, the definition transforms into what I call a 'daffynition'. The idea the Universe is put together like a machine is an example of a daffynition. Now if I were to claim the Universe is a flower that would be a daffynition. The most I can say is that it is more like a flower than it is like a machine. This thinking is an example of what I refer to as a Dictionary approach wherein the dictionary one person uses is assumed to be the dictionary all use and in the end, all this does is turn an Icon into an Idol. My proposal is that we use what I call a Thesaurus approach. In the long run, it Does Not Matter that one person sees God, another sees G-d, yet another sees Allah, someone else sees Krishna, and so on, we are seeing the same Central Reality that is the source of all images. Atonement is

7

different than Enlightenment only in the definitions, just as Chinese and Spanish are different languages. Whether one views the Golden Rule from 'do unto' or 'do not do unto', it still results the same state of behavior. Charity is Charity, whether it is performed from a Christian or a Buddhist worldview. Both the Christian and the Confucianist have religious sanctions to 'honor thy mother and father.' Wicca and Christianity both consider murder to be sinful.

By taking a dictionary approach to theology, one makes an Idol out of an Icon and is a degradation of the concept of -O-. A dictionary is Literal while a thesaurus is figurative. All religions agree that -O- is Infinite yet they all want to portray their particular theology as Literal Truth for All. The Figurative Truth is that some people see the Divine in the Christian, some in the Buddhist, some in the Hindu, some in the Islamic, and so on, images, in which each is true in a limited sense. Out of Infinite Compassion, -O- appears to each person in the image they need, which is the inspiration behind St. Paul and his 'becoming all things to all men.' It is theological hypocrisy to claim one the one hand that -O- is Infinite and on the other to claim to have the exclusive -O-image for all humanity. Belief in a -O-image of some form is not a delusion as some on the Scienceism side attempt to convince; it is an allusion to a deeper truth.

One problem with using the dictionary approach is that one falls into dualistic thinking, assuming the thing named 'body' is a different thing than the thing named 'mind'. Not only are they different, as the campfire story goes; they are fundamentally separate entities that have little to do with each other. An electron is neither 'particle', 'wave', nor 'wavicle'; it is something we know little about doing things we can almost talk about. Body is real, but only to a certain point. Mind is real, but only to a certain point. What we call 'Yang' and what we call 'Yin' is the surface of what we call 'Tao' and that is what is Real. That which we call 'body' and that which we call 'mind' are the same energy doing different thingies at the same time just like 'particles' and 'waves' are.

The trouble with traditional dualistic thinking is the assumption one Or the other point of view is The Truth©. Many cogent arguments have been given to prove that mind is a byproduct of body and many have been given that prove the opposite point of view. What these arguments fail to take into account is that they are talking about different aspects of the same reality and not different realities; it is quite obvious the head and tail of a coin are not different things, but different faces of the same thing. We think of the 'dividing line' as a barrier that none may cross rather than a point of linguistic agreement for the sake of communication. Yes, the mental is different than the physical, but that does not mean they are different things in essence. Body is the physical aspect while mind is the nonphysical aspect of an undifferentiated Oneness. It matters not where one looks in the schools of dualistic thinking, the result is some form of monism, which I submit is a lopsided point of view. The 'mind only' and the 'body only' arguments both have 'yes, but . . . ' issues reminding me of the Yin-Yang symbol wherein each contain a bit of the other.

This is the beauty of the whole shebang, no matter how much we know, we are beginners and our knowledge is just as incomplete as when we started. I'm not degrading knowledge when I call it 'incomplete'; I'm merely recognizing that knowledge is finite while Oneness is infinite. Not only is Reality much grander than we imagine, it is grander than we *can* imagine. The problems within traditional dualism and monism come from our concept of metaphysics; in which said issues are considered 'outside' or 'beyond' the phenomenal world. In one sense, this is true; the Ultimate is 'outside' as it *contains* all this. I submit this is a limited view as the Ultimate is also an 'inside' thingie, for the Ultimate is *contained by* all this. The Ultimate is not a state to which all things aspire but the Source from which all things arise. The Dualist approach claims the 'sides' of the issue are fundamentally separate Realities and the Monist answer claims only one of them is truth. Where these approaches fail is in not realizing the images are allusions of a deeper truth, not The Truth Itself©.

The biggest problem with the 'name is the thing' approach is that we end up with silliness like the 'Death of God' philosophical argument and this latest round of 'God Delusion' stuff. This is but another round in the Clash Between Science and Religion with both sides claiming the *sole* right to speak for all of us. On the Theological side is the claim the Biblical description is the Only Truth while the Scienceism side claims that because Science discounts *some* theological reasoning about God, He therefore does not exist. It is hubristic to take the stance that any one image is the sole truth for -O- is the Source of all images; He is one and the same time, the God of the Bible and the Tao of the Tao Te Ching. The thing we ignore is that our images are little more than Finite attempts at defining an Infinity in the same manner the ingredients are not the cake. It is not the case that we must choose either side of this nonissue generated by a few knee jerk radicals for one can believe the Theory of Evolution to be a campfire story about Hindu reincarnation.

One can have a theological outlook that is not Biblical and a scientific outlook that is not Atheistic. I take a radical monism stance, as in 'the Many are emanations of the One', although I use radical nondualism reasoning, as in 'not One, not Two'. It all depends on how we look at 'One'; from the *exclusive* point of view, it is singular and from the *inclusive* view, it is manifold. It is radical monotheism as in '-O- is the Source of all -O-images'; all images are *re*presentations of the Unnamable. -O- and man are not separate realities but two of the infinite aspects of this same Reality. Mind and body are not two realities unto themselves, but two more of the infinite patterns of this same Reality. Likewise, the so-called dichotomy of -O- and Nature is a matter of linguistics and not Reality itself. It stands to reason that as -O- is the inside

inside of everything, it is reasonable to assume Holiness at the core of all there is. The Nature of the Physical Realm is one of the many emanations of the Divine Source, just as Human Nature is an emanation of the Divine Soul. Neither is 'flawed' because of the temporality, for as the Buddhists say, 'all compounded things are subject to dissolution.'

I submit a mistake takes place within traditional philosophical thinking with the adoration of the Spiritual and the denigration of the Material. These 'sides' are not opposites, but compliments like a pair of wings and we need both to fly. Without the Physical, as we know it, we would not have the Spiritual, as we know it. We set our hopes on either eternal life in Heaven or eternal nonlife in Nirvana because of this attitude and in doing so; we deny the greatest gift that -O- has given, life. In other words, there is no *There* we can go to for escape. Granted there is a bit of pain and suffering involved with living, but for the most part, it is enjoyable and that is what we should be paying attention to. Much of this pain and suffering has been eliminated and/or reduced through increased knowledge about the causes and how to alleviate the associated problems and this will continue into the future.

It seems to me that traditional thinking takes a wrong-headed approach to the question of what it means to be a Human Being. If one does not take to Biblical Literalness, the story that we were 'created in His Image' can be understood 'Humans are Living Icons of The Most Holy.' Our temporality is not the result of Original Sin, as some campfire stories go, but is a natural result of existing as physical beings. It is a mistake to consider physicality a burden to bear, as other campfire stories go, but a joy to experience. As far as the campfire story of evolution goes, the whole story falls short by thinking of it as 'the descent of man' when the whole thing started when the One evolved into whatever evolved into matter and energy from which stars evolved, which in the third generation begat humanity. Carl Sagan put it nicely by telling the story 'we are star stuff come alive.'

If you do not ascribe to a spiritual campfire story, look at it from a secular position, Humans are the Universes' method of being alive and aware. It seems that here on Earth, the whole point of the evolutionary process was to come up with living, self-aware beings. A whole bunch of time and energy went into producing us and we waste it bitching and moaning about trivial matters. You may say this is all trivial as physicality is meaning*less* as it is based on randomness but I say it is all meaning*ful* as there are patterns within the chaos, one of which gave rise to the improbability of you and I discussing it. This appears to me a magical trick of supernormal proportions and is about the most awesome thought I can almost wrap my mind around.

One of these campfire stories has us as Living Icons and another has us as the Universe become alive and aware. These stories paint a better image of humanity as far as I'm concerned than the ones of us as either 'fallen creatures' or as 'mere flukes', as the two most popular stories of the West go. Inherent in these stories is that we are not visitors to this vale of tears just passing through on a one-time visit but rather recurring guest actors. This attitude of being visitors with eternal souls has always thrown me for a loop for despite all the stories of our probable destination post-death; there is not a word about where we come from in our pre-birth state. If we are eternal, why is it that we have no memories of all that time between the beginning and when we were born? If our soul comes into existence at our conception, that kinda rules out the idea of being 'eternal', does it not? While it just may turn out to be true that consciousness is a byproduct of the material, the idea that we are not intimately connected with the physical realm shows lack of imagination on the part of the Scienceism Literalist.

It is my contention this attitude of non-relatedness is the primary reason there is a profound lack of environmentalism in theology and most science; this goes back to the dualist misunderstanding mentioned earlier. More than anything else, it is a failure to connect -O- and Nature that leads to this lack, promoting a false dichotomy between Sacred and Secular. We treat it as if it were an either/or thingie not realizing it is actually a goeswith thingie like the heads and tails of a coin. One way of imaging Physical Reality is as the 'body' of -O- and therefore, Holy. From a purely Material perspective, the universe is what it is because we are what we are. If, for example, humans had no perception of red, the description of the visual universe would be much different than it is now. The campfire story of Human awareness being a one-time flash in the pan ignores the idea of the Conservation Laws and that the whole universe recycles. Likewise, the campfire story of the Human soul as being an individual, eternal thingie that is totally separate from physical reality ignores the idea that the spiritual is known through the material.

While it is true to say 'we are created in His image', the Truth is that -O- is not a white male being. It would be just as true to say 'we were created in Her image', but -O- is not a black female being either. Christianity has a grain of truth in the campfire story of Incarnation, but limits the occasion to a one-time happening while Hinduism has a grain of truth in the campfire story of Avatar but limits it to -O- sending one only in times of great need. As the Central Reality, -O- is Incarnate in each of us, giving us the status of Living Icons, or avatars. There are responsibilities that come with our status as Living Icons. To act as if one were the *only* person to be -O- incarnate is to miss the point that you are just as equal an Icon as I am as is our friend over there. My treating you with disrespect would be a showing of disrespect to the -O-head within you as well as to the -O-head within me.

This is why I take such a strong stance against what I call the Theology of Hate, for each and every Human is a Living Icon of -O-, deserving as much respect as one demands for oneself. I get particularly perturbed when violent movements attempt to wrap themselves in the mantle of religion. How can -O- hate that which He is the Central Reality? There has been nothing in my mystical experiences that even hints that -O- would condone the killing of innocents to further a cause and I submit that the killing of innocents in the 'Name of God' is a major sin. As far as I'm concerned, the violence committed in the name of religion is politically motivated criminal behavior and deserves to be treated as such. At this point, it Does Not Matter who started the atrocities, what Does Matter is stopping the transgressions of civil behavior of all sides.

I realize I have covered a lot of ground with little explanation, for which I apologize, but I wanted to give you a headline tour of the conversations that follow. I hope you enjoy reading these little ditties as much as I enjoyed in having, then later recreating, them. (As close as I could.) Be forewarned that these topics are never-ending for there is no way to weave a net of words tight enough to catch that which is Infinitely small. One cannot label the Infinite with a Finite just as one cannot swallow the Pacific in one gulp, but this is not to imply that we are on a mission of failure. Think of it like a type of triangulations where one points at the target from many angles.

Neomonism

x>x>The Dictionary Approach gives one the idea of contradictions while the Thesaurus Approach gives one the idea of Paradox.
x>You keep returning to the idea of paradox. Why is that?

At the preverbal level, the experience of Divine Union makes perfect sense; it is when we go silly and try talking about it that trouble arises. In one sense, talking about the Unity of -O- and Human is the same sort of thing as talking about the Unity of Particle and Wave. A Particle is the physical manifestation of a wave pattern, a Human is a manifestation of -O-, and a Noun is the mental freezing of Verb. I feel that our habit of assuming that we all have the same mental dictionary is what contributes the most to the quandary of paradox.

The paradox does not appear until we try to talk about our experiences of Unity with the expectation that all involved will understand the concept of 'Unity' equally. We have a tendency to leave our thesaurus out of the conversation because we care more about knowledge than we do gnowledge. In other words the Isness takes precedent over Islikeness, especially when it comes to the topic of -O-.

x>x>What is needed is a middle path between taking the symbolic as concrete and ignoring the symbolic altogether.
x>Are you proposing that we allow the Mythic as a valid source of knowledge?

What I am proposing is that we recognize that rather than representing reality, the Scientific Theories and Mythic explanations are *re*presentations of reality. The Mythic looks at reality from one angle, the Scientific from another, but they are both looking at the same reality. Look at it this way, one can view a picture of the Andromeda Galaxy taken in visible light, one taken in Infrared, and one taken by a radio telescope; each is a view of the same object taken from a 'different angle', as it were. The view from the radio telescope is no less a real view of the Galaxy than is the visible light view and one view does not automatically cancel out the other views.

I am reminded of the story of the blind men and the elephant. In the story, a group of men are attempting to "see" what an elephant looks like by feeling various areas of the body. One has the trunk and one has an ear and each think that represents the elephant in toto. The overwhelming majority of us are stuck in the same type of argument these men are in – "On my careful study of the elephant, I deem it is like a fan." is one pronouncement and "On my careful study of the elephant, I deem it is like a rope." is the other persons' pronouncement. This comes from concentrating on the differences. Yes, an elephants' ear is like a fan and the trunk is like a rope, but neither the trunk nor the ear either alone or together comprises the entire elephant. During their discussion, they describe all the features and an important aspect is missed - the elephant is gray in color.

x>x>What I am proposing is that we recognize that rather than representing reality, the Scientific Theories and Symbolic/Mythic explanations are *re*presentations of reality. The Symbolic/Mythic looks at reality from one angle, the Scientific from another, but they are both looking at the same reality.
x>What if the Mythic and the Scientific do not agree, which are we to hold as final authority?

I don't think we should hold either as Final Authority; they should balance each other in a seamless unity with the whole ball of wax being a *re*presentation of That Which Is. This is a Dynamic balance, not a Static one, as there is an ongoing balance between positive and negative, good and evil, light and dark, ad nauseam. The Uncertainty Principle works here as well - to misquote, "The more we know about Scientific, the less we know about Mythic." I feel that the Scientific and the Mythic aspects of understanding should complement each other; anything else would be like an odorless rose. I feel that as long as we continue thinking there must be a Final authority between those two choices alone, we are missing the bigger picture.
Many of those who are of the Scientific only point of view of reality claim to be atheistic when in my mind, all they have accomplished is the replacement of one -O- image with another. Rather than not believing in -O-, I feel it is a nonbelief in the typical Western misunderstandings of -O- as an outside agency that controls every aspect of reality, and as far as I am concerned, the Scientific worldview is Deism without the Deity. The traditional 'Scientific only' misunderstanding of reality leaves one with the image of reality as a mechanism that performs according to certain Laws, which is fine for pragmatic purposes, but leaves something to be desired on the esthetic level.
Like the Scientific, the Mythic has many theories to choose, from the Western image of -O- as a Personal Being to the Eastern image of -O- as Beingness that is the Source of all images. The problem with this is the number - which of these

do we hold as final authority to use as a balance to the Scientific? It seems to me there are three basic answers to the question of the existence of -O-.

One can say "No" and walk the path of Atheism. I have never seen a true Atheist though, as those who claim to be Atheists have really done nothing more than replace one -O- concept with another. Most who claim to be Atheistic are so, in my opinion, merely due to rejection of the Biblical image of -O- and ignorance of other theologies.

An answer of "Maybe" leads one to the path of Agnosticism. An Agnostic, in the modern connotation of the term, holds there is not enough evidence at present to either prove or disprove the existence of -O-. One side of this path has those who believe "Maybe Yes" and on the other side are those who believe "Maybe No". The former are considered "Soft Agnostics" and the latter are considered "Hard Agnostics". The agnostic stance properly speaking, is not about the existence or nonexistence of -O- in as much as it is about whether or not we humans will ever have complete knowledge of -O-. There are examples of religious agnosticism in both East and West - the philosophy of Sunyata in Buddhism and apophetic knowledge in Christianity, for example. Agnosticism, in the technical sense of the term, is knowing without knowledge, a state I call gnowledge.

There are many variations of the "Yes" answer. The two basic "Yes" answers are either dualistic or nondualistic. Although the proponents of the Dualistic path claim their theology posits an Infinite, their Divine is, in fact Finite, as the theology posits a fundamental and inseparable dichotomy between -O- and the physical realm. The Nondualistic paths posit an identification of -O- in the world (Pantheism) with an anthropomorphic theology or through the world (Panentheism) with a nonanthropomorphic theology.

Although the Pantheistic path has the appearance of belonging on the Dualistic path, it is so only on the surface. For example, the Hindu Tradition has all the surface appearance of being Pantheistic, but when one dives beneath the symbolism, it is Panentheistic. On the Dualistic paths, we have the image of the Active and the Passive -O-. In the former, -O- takes charge of everything, controlling history and the hearts of men. The Passive -O- has not been involved in the physical realm since Creation (Deism).

There is no real difference in essence between the Dualistic images of -O- as Deity and the Nondualistic image of the Tao. Both are images of a Reality that is responsible for setting all this in motion and letting things follow their own nature. The Dualistic Anthropomorphic concept of -O- as involved in history is really not that much different than the Nondualistic Anthropomorphic concept expressed in Hinduism of Brahma sending Himself as an Avatar when needed.

It seems logical to assume that the existence of so many who say "Yes" to the existence of -O- would be cause for celebration. The major difference in the two "Yes" answers is that the Dualistic answer is "This is what -O- Is" while the Nondualistic answer is "This is what -O- Is Like". The major similarity is "-O- is One." much like in the story of the elephant talked about earlier.

x>x>In any religion there are two traditions; one is theological, one is mystical.
x>Could you explain this a little more?

The Theological is the Messenger side and the Mystical is the Message side of the tradition. Look at the difference between Theravada and Mahayana Buddhism, the former sticks to what The Buddha actually said, while the latter explores what the Buddha meant. (While this somewhat overstates the case, it is a valid example.) In Creedal Christianity, the person of Jesus must be accepted as Lord and Savior while Mystical Christianity would concern itself with the persona of Christ.
One argument we see from those on the Theological side of the fence in the West is that mystics want to throw out the "Traditional" understanding. In my humble opinion, to suggest the Mystical approach is opposed to the Literal approach is to miss the point entirely - the Mystical approach compliments the Literal, just like the Mythic compliments the Scientific. I submit the Theological grew from the Mystical in the same manner that Science grew from Myth.

x>x>Come now, both of you. We all know that a 'reasonable mysticism' is a contradiction in terms. Reason is not sloppy and mysticism is not precise.
x>Mysticism without reason soon becomes a sloppy emotionalism. Reason without mysticism is dry and uninspiring.

I fail to understand the need in the West to reduce everything to a "this vs. that" oversimplification so that one side can yell "This" and the other side can yell "That". If "Wave" is the reality, what in the heck is it doing behaving like a "Particle" and what are we going to do with this thingie we label "Wavicle"? When we make an attempt to nail everything down in an either/or type of classification, we end up looking silly, especially when we end up talking about a Platypus.
In looking for something on one side of the equation as final authority is to take a lopsided view of things, when what we need to take is a balanced approach. Most people in the West tend to think along a straight line when a straight line is nothing more than a circle turned on its side. We need to turn our thinking on its side, as it were, and look for dynamic balance in our understanding of Reality. The Mythic is just as important as the Scientific. What is needed

is a complimentary balance between what we know and what we gno about Reality.

x>x>I do not think we should hold either as final authority, they should balance each other in a seamless unity with the whole ball of wax being a *re*presentation of That Which Is.

x>Science and Religion are fundamental opposites. We have all heard the statements by Scientists about Science proving there is no God.

The Scientific understanding does not deny the existence of -O- per se; it calls into question the traditional Western image of -O-, which is the root of the problem causing some people to assume there is a fundamental dichotomy between Science and Religion. With the exception of Biblical Literalists, there is no dichotomy between the concept of Evolution and a figurative understanding of the Biblical Creation story. Randomness and uncertainty in Quantum Physics poses no opposition to Buddhist and Taoist Philosophy. The cycles found in the natural world (Water, Carbon, Nitrogen, etc.) pose no threat to the Hindu ideas of Rebirth and a cyclic nature of Reality.

It seems to me the biggest obstacle in this issue is that most people tend to think of -O- in traditional Western terms, as if the traditional Western image is the Absolute Truth™ of the Matter. The majority of people I talk to have this idea that if the Biblical -O-image is wrong, there is, ipso facto, no -O-. This is based on ignorance of Eastern Theology and mystical experience in general. When one looks at the writings of the great mystics and the great physicists, it is hard to tell the difference between the two, much like the skin of the elephant being all the same color whether it is the trunk, leg, or tail.

The publication of books like "The Tao of Physics" generated a bit of discussion about how the purpose of these books was to use Science to prove Eastern Religious thought. Whether this was the purpose or not, they did a good job of using the ideas of Science to illuminate the ideas of Eastern Theology. One issue I do not remember being discussed was how they also illuminated mystical insight in general. I cannot remember the number of times I have been reading something about Quantum Physics and have had the feeling the things they were talking about had much in common with something I had felt in mystical experience. The paradoxes of Quantum Physics are not that different than the paradoxes of theology and understanding in both fields comes through being comfortable with paradox.

x>x>x>Science and Religion are fundamental opposites. We have all heard the statements by Scientists about Science proving there is no God.

x>x>The Scientific understanding does not deny the existence of -O- per se . . . It seems to me the biggest obstacle in this issue is that most people tend to think of -O- in traditional Western terms, as if the traditional Western image is the Absolute Truth™ of the Matter.

x>I have talked long enough with you to get the impression that you aren't really happy with Eastern images either.

Heck, I'm not happy with any image; if I thought -O- could be captured in an image, I would be disappointed. After all, -O- is infinite, how the heck are we gonna slap an image on an infinity? The Tao is an adequate image philosophically but I have to say that it leaves something to be desired symbolically and the same can be said about the Buddhist philosophies of Sunyata and Tathata. In their own ways, these images are as dry as the images proposed by modern Science. Since I have started walking the path of mysticism, I have had a few experiences of the Divine, and there are certain themes, God who is Totally Other, -o- who is Totally Self, and That which is neither and both at the same time. The only term I can think to type that covers this aspect would be -O-. When speaking, the sound of each is the same so there really isn't a problem.

One of the experiences is of God. This is the Totally Other, Majestic and awe inspiring aspect that we approach in all humility. This is the God of Pascal's fire, the King of Kings, the Holy Father, the I AM, the Tathata, the Yang, the particulate aspect of reality, etc. My experience of this aspect has always taken on the flavor of There is nothing but this. This experience of the Divine puts me on my knees. God is so majestic how dare I not be reverent? All I can do is put my forehead in the dust of the ground and await His Command. I look around me at all this and the beauty is nothing compared to the utter wonder of God. This is my stern yet loving Father who is not averse to slapping my wrist if needs be yet is also willing to provide me with everything I need. All that, taken together, is not this, no matter how holy it appears.

Another aspect is -o-, the Total Self of reality that is humble and we approach with dignity. This is the Divine Mother, Sunyata, Yin and the wave aspect of reality, and also the I AM. My experience of this has always taken on the flavor of AND, Thou art That. This experience of the Divine fills me with Joy. -o- is the Mother of all creation, how dare I not be reverent? She is the One I come running to when I stub my toe on this path. She kisses it and makes it feel better then tells me to keep a better eye on where I'm going while She fixes Hot Chocolate. All that taken together, is this, no matter how base it appears.

There are times, however, that the experience cannot be talked about in terms of gender. Plainly and simply, the terms do not apply. A sense of Persona is present yet there is no hint of Personality. The experience is something that just cannot be put into words. This experience of the Divine fills me with the wonder of a young child. -O- is the Source of all creation, how can I be reverent enough?

There are times when God the Father appears and times when -O- the Mother shows up in mystical experience and there are times when -O- comes for a visit. Each persona has that which is feminine about them and each person has that which is masculine about them, but, in and of themselves, neither aspect is the whole person. If we humans, who partake of the Divine image can have these two complimentary aspects yet not be bound by either, how much more so the Divine?

I am not saying that when God shows up, I see a Masculine Being. When I talk about -o- the Mother, I'm not talking about a Feminine Being and -O- is not some sort of luminous Jell-O that somehow permeates the universe. To consider the Divine to be a being with a personality is silly at the least, and idolatrous at the worst. Imaging the Divine as some kind of substance that is all through the universe is just as silly. These are merely ways to describe how the experience feels to me, not how the Divine actually is in the ultimate sense of the term. The words and concepts behind them are nothing more than pointers toward That Which Cannot Be Spoken.

No matter what type of experience I have had, each one has left the impression of a Living Reality, even when that term is woefully inadequate to the task at hand.

x>x>There are times when God the Father appears and times when -o- the Mother shows up in mystical experience and there are times when -O- comes for a visit. Each persona has . . .

x>I am curious Dino - what exactly is the context and differences in which you use "God", "-o-", and "-O-"?

I use the term God for the times my experience of the Divine has what can only be described as Yang, or masculine, like the Pascal's Fire type of experience where the Divine Light is reflected by the universe. The -o- experience is the Yin, or Feminine. It too is like Pascal's Fire; only the Divine Light is not a reflection by the universe but an emanation of the universe. The -O- experience cannot be described as Yin or Yang, reflection or emanation, masculine or feminine, self or other, as none of these dualistic terms apply - it is pure fire.

I used to live in Mendocino County, in Northern California. One day while walking through a meadow in the back county, the meadow suddenly lit up as if Creation had just occurred - the perfection of the meadow was a reflection of the perfection of G-d. Another time, the meadow lit up, but from the "inside", as it were, and the perfection of -O- was shown by the perfection of the meadow.

Yet another time, there was Divine Light, both reflected and emanated. It seemed to me as if the Divine was saying "I Am all this and more".

One thing I do have to admit is that over the years, I have been having less of the God and -o- experiences. As a result, I have a hard time using anthropomorphic language when discussing -O- with people. I know full well that people (In Western Traditions) think my saying that reality is both a reflection of His Power and an emanation of Her Grace makes me look foolish. I have a hard time with dualistic language as well as -O- transcends the concepts of Emmanance and Immanence – it is equally valid to take the Hindu approach of negativism, as it is to take the Buddhist approach of positivism.

One of the biggest problems I have with traditional Western Theology is that the feminine aspect of -O- is suppressed past the point of denial. Even before I could articulate this I knew there was something incomplete about the daffynitions I had heard in church about -O-s' Attributes. Yes, there is an aspect of -O- that is masculine, but that is not the entirety of -O-, just as a male is not the entirety of humanity.

x>x>I know full well that people (In Western Traditions) think my saying that reality is both a reflection of His Power and an emanation of Her Grace makes me look foolish. I have a hard time with dualistic language as well as -O- transcends the concepts of Emmanance and Immanence - it is equally valid to take the Hindu approach of negativism, as it is to take the Buddhist approach of positivism.

x>It sounds to me like you are using Eastern Theology and your private Mystical philosophy to justify the concept of Modalism and the Religion of Science.

Modalism is one Philosophy that comes close to describing the Reality behind the experience and Science does illuminate both Eastern Theology and my Mystical philosophy, but I am not saying that any particular One holds The Truth™. The Philosophy of Modalism is not carried out to its logical conclusion of each human being a monad of -O-. As I have said earlier, the Religion of Science is nothing more than Deism without the Deity, which to me is a dry substitute with no internal life.

As far as I am concerned, these kinds of comments and complaints are nothing but emotional smokescreens for the real issue, which is "How shall we image this Reality we call -O-?" The radicals on the Western Religionist side wish to maintain the Biblical Image while the radicals on the Scientific side maintain no -O- at all and both sides make so much noise that other options are drowned out in the din. I find it somewhat amusing that people who find themselves involved in this argument rarely mention that no complaints are heard from Eastern Religions. Even more amusing is that we hear complaints from both sides of this issue when things are said comparing Modern Science and Eastern Philosophy favorably.

Why all too many of the Western Religionists complain is understandable, it is their knee-jerk reaction to anything that favors another image of -O- or makes Science look like a valid competitor. Complaints from the Scientific Community confuse me somewhat as the original aim of Science was to learn about -O- through learning about the Universe. One would think they would be pleased to find theologies that compliment their findings rather than spout a knee-jerk reaction against anything that has the appearance of Religion.

Why the issue evolved to a spitting contest of whether -O- is the Biblical daffynition or there is no -O- is beyond my understanding. It is absurd to assume that one must have either a Religious or a Scientific view of Reality. If one is willing to leave aside the insistence that our image of -O- be Biblical, one can discover a Reality behind reality that can only be described as Spiritual. One must be willing as well to toss aside the Universe as Machine image of Scientism and see the universe as an Organic, Spiritual, and Living Reality.

I highly doubt that I have been promoting the "Religion of Science". Scientism is just as Incomplete as Religionism, only it is Incomplete from another direction. The Agnostic school of thought is just as necessary here as it is in the Field of Religion. By this, I am not saying that we should ignore the validity of the Scientific outlook, only that we should not carry the outlook to where it is ineffective. Have you ever considered how boring it must be to have Total Knowledge in All Things That Are and Will Be? There will never be an end to the Scientific Process as there will always be something to learn, but this does not mean that empirical knowledge is all there is to the Total Picture.

x>x>Scienceism is just as Incomplete as Religionism, only it is Incomplete from another direction. The Agnostic school of thought is just as necessary here as it is in the Field of Religion.

x>What you are saying, then, is that we cannot have complete knowledge in any field of study. It sounds dismal and skeptical to me. What sense is there in studying anything then?

Far from dismal, my efriend, but a sheer delight. Think about it for a while, do you not find learning to be exciting? Maybe I am a bit strange (MAYBE???), but I find learning to be a blast. I have been working through a Temp agency for over 20 years and although the pay is not great and the benefits are little, if any, I have had a blast learning many new things. Among the things I have learned is being a sheet metal machinist working with tolerances of .0001", Assembly of medical devices, Shipping and Receiving in various warehouse style companies, ISO 9000 level inspection of tubing to be used in the Nuclear

Industry, tree trimming, and working in the kitchen at an airport. I have built knives and have experience in a mailroom.

I cannot remember where, but I once read an essay by Lewis Thomas, about how the Introduction to Science classes should be titled "The Things We Do Not Know". Along that train of thought, I would add that one of the textbooks should be "The Wisdom of Insecurity", by Alan Watts. Science has gone through the same kind of internal belching in clinging to graven images of the mind that Religion has and needs to pay attention to the same message. In all the various assignments I have had as a temp, the one thing I have noticed is that if a person is burned out on the job, it is because they know all about it and have nothing new to learn. One way of putting it is that the magic goes out of life when one knows it all.

What can be more dismal than having Complete Knowledge? Can you imagine how boring that must be after a while? If there is any image of Hell that scares me, it is one of an eternity of knowing everything and every event beforehand. Sure, one can have a safer life if one knows what is coming, but, how long could one remain tied to apron strings before one wanted a taste of adventure? I would prefer to walk around a corner to see either a beautiful sunset or a charging dragon without foreknowledge, thank you. This does not mean that I am against knowledge, as much as it may sound to some people - it is nice to know the chances of meeting a dragon are less than seeing a sunset.

As for being "skeptical", yes it is, skeptical of the Wisdom of Complete Knowledge™. Giving up the Magical Universe is not worth the trade off involved as far as I am concerned, for we live neither in the Predestined universe of the Traditional Western Religions nor the Mechanical Universe of Traditional Western Science. The discovery of new aspects of physical reality is just as exciting as discovery of new aspects of Ultimate Reality and I submit it is this excitement that gives us a sense of curiosity about the world around us. One can be a Skeptic without being negative, by the way.

To be dismayed by the idea that one cannot Know ultimate reality is to miss the point that no matter what, there is always something more to learn. If there is any One trait that has marked our success as a species, it is our constant striving for new knowledge about the universe; coming to Full and Total Knowledge would mean an end to that success and herald the beginning of our decline. Sometimes I wonder if people actually sit down and consider what it would be like to have full and complete knowledge of each and every little thing now and into the future. How can the magic survive if one can never surprise our loved one with a dozen roses?

All too many of us look at the unknown with fear, which I feel is a mistake as venturing into the unknown is what human history is all about. From our modest start, we have come to colonize just about the entire planet. Our medical knowledge has advanced from blaming demons to targeting the cause of disease. Our technical expertise has progressed from campfires to microwave ovens and from bone tipped spears to nuclear tipped ICBMs. Much of what was unknown in the past is now known and there is just as much to learn and be surprised about.

x>x>To be dismayed by the idea that one cannot Know ultimate reality is to miss the point that no matter what, there is always something more to learn. If there is any One trait that has marked our success as a species, it is our constant striving for new knowledge . . .
x>This is a bit confusing. Earlier it seemed as if you were talking down Knowledge. Now it seems as if you are saying it is a good thing.

What I am talking down is how we have a tendency to take a little bit of an answer and extend it beyond its' proper sphere, as exemplified by the chatter earlier about the isms leading to black nosed Buddhas. There is just too much about Reality that is unknown for us to think we can use what little we do know to use as a club to beat up on those who have other ideas.
My complaint is not in the search itself, but in some of the things we have accomplished with the knowledge. Knowledge (The Answer) has become the Holy Grail rather than the Search (The Question) and I submit it has much to do with the success of Newtonian Mechanics. It seemed only logical to conclude that all that was left to Science was the filling in of the blanks. This had a spillover into Western Theology in that Newtonian Mechanics validated the Western Image of –O- as the Watchmaker Who Knew How It Was All Put Together. Unfortunately, some of the filling in did not match predictions, which led to a questioning of prevailing theories, both of the Scientific and Theological Images. The Quantum Revolution in Science has had its counterpart in Religion as well. One of the key ideas in early modern science was that by knowing the Universe, one could come to know -O-, and as knowledge of the Universe increased, the less it validated the Traditional Western Image of -O-.
For some reason, this got turned into a "Death of -O-" movement, as if the only choice of -O-image was that offered by the West. All that has been called into question is the Certainty of our Images, not Reality Itself. The Uncertainty Principle shows the fallacy of imaging -O- as knowing each and every little thing about the Universe for if one knows the position of an electron, one cannot know anything about its momentum. Black holes violate conservation laws unless it is shown that white holes are their counterparts; for every left-handed black hole, there should be a right-handed white hole, in other words.
What has Certainty given us in the long run? For many years, whites were certain they were superior, but all that did was lead to much strife in the area

of racial unrest. This idea of different races within the Human Species and is a consequence of how humans have a tendency to look at an issue from the surface and declare that to be "The Truth, the Whole Truth, and Nothing but the Truth™". All humans are the same for the overwhelming part; the difference between each of us is relatively minor.

For most of our existence we were certain that Earth was the Center of the Universe, look at all the trouble that came about when scientists started talking about the Earth as the body moving while the Sun was stationary. Now we realize there is no one stationary object in the entire Universe. The history of Western Science showed the Fallacy of Certitude when Quantum Mechanics butted heads with Newtonian Mechanics; what had been assumed to be a predictable machine turned out to be semi-rational, semi-chaotic, and full of surprises. The one thing we should have drawn from looking back at the history of any field of study is that there is always more to learn.

Neotheology

The other day, I was having a conversation with a friend in which she said that she assumed that because I do not believe in the Biblical God, I'm Atheist. It is a sad but true statement that people assume that if one does not accept the Biblical Image of God, one does not believe in -O- in any image.

x> . . . a nobler image of God . . .
x>What do you mean by a nobler image?

I doubt if people stop to think about the image of -O- (The spelling '-O-' is pronounced "God".) they present to people of other Faiths, especially the more right wing believers. One thing I have come to realize through this mystical path is that my appreciation of the Divine grows deeper and awesome has become AWESOME. My point is that some of the things that are said about -O- are downright blasphemous. Some of the things people say about -O- make Him out to be the Ultimate Neighborhood Bully and Someone To Fear.

Something I commented on in our conversation about the Theology of Hate was my opposition to this idea that -O- 'takes sides' in our conflicts. If I were to believe in -O- as A Being, I imagine the idea of warfare would make -O- cry, and when I think about that, I feel like I gotta go change my pants. At the core of all Religions is the idea that -O- loves equally, so how can anyone say 'Dad loves me more than you' and think it is true? There has been nothing in my experience that gives me the slightest hint that -O- is petty enough to get involved on one side or another in our squabbles for, as it is written, the rain falls on the Just as well as on the Unjust. Going on the assumption that -O- is the cause of all events, we must assume that He caused both sides of the argument to come about. Can one say with certainty that G-d is on the side of Israel or that Allah is on the side of Palestine, or should we say that both sides sadden -O-?

The things some people say about -O- after natural disasters are so blasphemous, I'm surprised -O- doesn't strike them down. How dare the imams tell someone a tsunami that kills thousands of innocents was punishment from Allah? Likewise for a Christian to claim that an earthquake that killed hundreds was God's Punishment for those Hindus worshipping "False Gods." These events were triggered by natural events, not a vengeful God, G-d, or Allah, and if World

History been a bit different, the victims could have been Christian. Blaming the disaster following a volcanic eruption on God is no different than placing the blame on the god of the mountain. I imagine disasters like that make -O- cry. One of the things that started me on this path was the difference in the -O-images of the church my grandparents attended and the one my mother sent us kids to. The former talked of the Loving God in the image of The Good Shepherd while the latter exhorted the Vengeful and Jealous God who demanded Retribution. Although I could not express it at the time, the former image made more sense as the first of my mystical experiences included a sense of being Infinitely Loved. There has been no doubt in my mind since the first experience that -O- is, the doubt comes in daffyfining what -O- is, although that is an awkward way to put it. The trouble for mystics is that language fails to convey more than the barest essentials of the meaning. On the one hand, it makes sense to talk about -O- as if He were a what because that is how we understand concepts. On the other hand, however, we make a mistake by thinking the words relate to an actual whatness.

Perhaps the biggest mistake is in thinking of -O- as a being in a highly glorified version of how we are beings. We yak about Him sitting on the Heavenly Throne as if this were an actual state of affairs. We are told that humans could not survive a face to Face meeting. I don't think people realize the Idolatry that comes with this thinking for it replaces an Infinite Reality with a Finite Image. The -O-image each of us carries around is not a representation but a *re*presentation, which comes through in imagery and language that points and we make a mistake when we confuse the menu for the meal. Thinking of -O- as a being is one of those confusions, for if He is one type of being, He cannot be another, which by daffynition shows that He is Finite. We all agree that whatever it is we call -O- is Infinite; by daffynition, this rules out that He is a Particular Being. One reason Buddhists do not use the word is that it has a tendency to turn into an Idol wherein a Buddhist cannot use the word "God" without someone assuming they are talking about the Biblical God. It is more accurate to think of -O- as beingness rather than being, for as it is written, "It is enough that I AM." An Infinite can be all images at once as -O- is the source, rather than the image. One way to look at it is that light is a blend of all colors, not any one color in particular.

Have Christian theologians ever considered how the story of Satan looks to Nonchristians? As there is no being that is All Good, there is no being that is All Evil. There is the potential for good/positive along with the potential for bad/negative in the Balance of Reality, neither of which is a fundamental and total opposite from the other. Yes, the Material realm is looked down upon in many Nonchristian Religions, but it is not a realm contaminated by the Antigod. An All Powerful God could have prevented the rebellion of Lucifer and his minions, so why didn't He? If God is All Loving and All Knowing, why did He create a being that He knew would cause much heartbreak? There are no answers to these questions other than 'the mystery of God' and all the stories do is tarnish the concept of -O- by discussing the source of evil as a failed creation of God.

Related to the Satan story is the one about Eternal Damnation in Hell. Is Condemnation for being exactly as one was created to be the action of a Just God? This is not a noble action. Taking the story of my ultimate fate being determined long before I was born as true, I would rather spend my aftertime in Hell and stay true to what has been written on my heart. I'm not saying Christian theology is unique with the concept of Hell, they are unique in the Eternal part of the equation. In Eastern theology, once one has done the time for the crime, they are back on the path to spiritual evolution. Tied in with this story is the one about Original Sin. The way this story runs, death in humans is the result of this supposed act of disobedience by our supposed ancestress. Is the punishment of all humans for the act of one included in the meaning of Justness? In Eastern Theology, death is a natural outcome of life, for, as it is said, all things must come to an end.

The story that -O- created a creature that has one short physical life that goes with a supposedly eternal soul is beyond comprehension. I've heard some theologians talk as if humans were immortal up until Eve ate the apple, but I find that story hard to swallow. Everywhere we look in the Universe, we find that all things are eventually perishable, in a grand retelling of the Buddhist idea that all compounded things are subject to dissolution. No matter how many reincarnations the soul may go through, it would be rare for there to be a direct reincarnation. Once 'i' die, 'i' doubt that 'i' will be coming back to the party. There are too many cyclic systems in Reality for me to accept the story of life being a one-shot thingie. Just because a particle appears, there is no reason to assume it is the same particle as one that disappeared earlier. The energy within the 'two' particles is the same, just as what takes place within that which we call 'soul'. However, when I say 'soul', I'm not talking about an individual human soul, as most people image. There is only one soul and that is what the Christians misunderstand as the Holy Ghost. Although 'i' do not survive death, 'I' am not affected by death, appearing as another 'i' somewhere in Reality. This is somewhat like the Hindu story of the Avatar or the Buddhist concept of transmigration.

And so, to finally get back to your original question about a 'nobler image', I humbly submit that no image is noble enough. It seems, however, there is some kind of Divine Imperative written into the Human Psyche for a -O-image of some sort. (Maybe this is the meaning behind 'Written on one's heart.') As long as we must have a -O-image, let it be one that at least is worthy of the Title. The image of a God who condemns to Eternal Punishment in Hell for being exactly as He created that person to be during his one life is not noble. An image that has -O- giving as many chances to get it right as necessary is noble. Whatever this Reality we call by different names actually is, He is Creator of the Jew as much as He is of the Gentile.

No matter what, it rains on Islamic lands just as it rains on Jewish lands. Through His many names, He is worshipped as God by the Christians, G-d by the Jews, Brahman by the Hindu, and Allah by the Muslims, just to mention a few. When I think of the story about how all this is a single shot affair whenafter God will roll up everything and we humans will spend the rest of Eternity either sitting at The Feet of God or in Hell, I find it profoundly lacking in imagination, for surely a Reality worthy of the Title "God" could come up with something better than that.

x>x>I doubt if people stop to think about the -O-image they present . . . Some of the things people say about -O- . . .

x>Why should it bother you that some Christians, for example, portray a less than loving picture of their God? Does that not make your God look better?

This is the whole problem in a nutshell; it is not the case that I have one God and the Christians another.

My two major complaints about Western Theological thinking is the assumption that God, Allah, and G-d are different entities and that these entities are Beings. This is just as mistaken as the idea that Hinduism is populated with many separate gods in that one ends up confusing the menu with the meal. Taoists have the Tao and Christians have God, Buddhists have Dharmakaya and Muslims have Allah, Judaism has G-d and Hinduism has Brahman, (although 'have' and 'has' are wrong, for they imply 'owns') in actuality, what we have are but differing ways of talking about that which cannot be said.

You tell the story that God created the Heavens and the Earth and I tell a story about how the Tao is beneath all this. We are both telling differing stories about the same whatever it was that took place. The difference in our stories is like looking at the front, then the back of a tapestry, which is the truer side? You tell a story of God as Completely Outside while I tell one about -O- as Completely Inside, both of our tales hold a grain of truth. The story you tell is that God created humans in His Image and the one I tell is that -O- is manifested in our image. I agree with you that no one of us is God, for -O- is all of us. (Side comment - all too many Westerners confuse the 'I am -O-' idea of the East to mean 'I personally am God.')

It bothers me because in assuming we have "Different Gods", we reduce -O- from an Infinite to a Finite and make the Finite an Idol. Stories about a vengeful God make no sense to someone who sees -O- as all loving and I wanted to cry when religious leaders blamed the tsunami in Indonesia on -O-. One could blame it on Neptune or Poseidon and still be as far from the Truth. These stories about "God being on our side" in a conflict are patently absurd seeing as how -O- created the other side as well. As far as I'm concerned, the stories some people tell about "God Hates . . . " to be Blasphemous in the extreme and it saddens me that few speak out against the Theology of Hate. I'm bothered by this idea there is One True Religion, because if one is true the others must be false. This is hubristic and demeaning to Religion in general.

There are as many faces of -O- as there are people; St. Paul was not the originator of 'becoming all things to all men.' It is true that -O- is Completely Outside, for Nothing Is -O-. It is also true that -O- is Completely Inside for there is Nothing But -O-. One truth does not cancel out the other as neither is The Truth, which is -O- is both at the same time. Completely Outside is a Finite concept, Completely Inside is a Finite concept, but the Infinity that is -O- includes both. He is Outside while She is Inside while the Holy Spirit moves the Center. My point here is that each of us has a portion of the truth with our -O-image, but -O- is not limited to or by a single truth.

x>x>not "illusion" as in fake, but "allusion", that which points to a deeper truth.
x>What do you think about the idea within The God Delusion?

I have not read the book yet but I would be surprised if it was different in essence than all Scientism tirades against Religionism. Just as some in the Religionism camp are afraid of nonbiblical understanding, some in the camp of Scientism are afraid of a Theory of Reality that is not Strictly Rational. Both sides are equally guilty of diminishing That Which Is into something we can put into words - the former says "This is what happened" and the latter says "This is how it may have taken place" and the radicals of neither side can see they are discussing the same thing from different angles. If it wasn't for Biblical Literalness, "Let there be light" could be a wonderful mythos for the Big Bang.

As I've yapped about before, this spitting contest that has been going on between the Religionism and Scientism camps is mostly the result of a vocal radical few on either side. Discoveries in Science raise questions about Biblical Theology, causing a tiff between the camps: the Biblical Literalist 'searches the Book and thinks he has found life' and the proponent of Scientism (Science Literalist) confuses lack of evidence for the Biblical God to be lack of evidence for any -O-image. The search for a Grand Unified Theory may be a secular enterprise, but it is carried out with all the seriousness of religion, with Priests, Holy Sites and Consecrated Rituals.

Holding a Theory is no different than holding a Theology and in that respect; Science and Religion are different forms of the same enterprise. Having a

Religious -O-image is no more and no less delusional than holding a Scientism image. The Images themselves are allusional and the delusion is in thinking one of the images is Truth.

x>x>Discoveries in Science raise questions about Biblical Theology, causing a tiff between the camps: the Biblical Literalist 'searches the Book and thinks he has found life' and the proponent of Scientism (Science Literalist) confuses lack of evidence for the Biblical God to be lack of evidence for any -O-image.
x>At least you're an equal opportunity critic in this area.

Does the Uncertainty Principle question the existence of -O- or does it question a premise of the Biblical daffynition? Why does it mean that if the Biblical daffynition is wrong in some respects that all -O-images are wrong? The Biblical and Science Literalists are equally hubristic when they act as if they can speak for all of us in these matters. I agree with the idea of -O- but I disagree that the Biblical daffynition is Absolute Truth©. There is no reason to assume the Biblical Creation Story is more than headlines for the story of evolution. I agree with the concept of evolution but I do not agree with it being a blind, stupid process taking place in a blind and stupid Universe.
I find it somewhat amusing to listen to the arguments between the two camps. These people each make idols out of images and attempt to force all people to accept one or the other as Truth. The Bibleist says only X is true while the Scientism apologist says only Y is true and both fail to realize their respective images are irrelevant when it comes to Reality, which is at least A through Z. The former looks at Reality as a flawed creation and the latter sees it as a blind and stupid machine, both denying the inherent magical quality of Reality. One thing these people have in common as far as I'm concerned is a profound lack of imagination when it comes to the grandeur of their images of Reality.
Lack of acceptance of the Biblical campfire story of God does not necessarily mean that one has a lack of a -O-image altogether. One can accept the campfire story of evolution without accepting the mechanical image of the Universe. There is truth in the Bibleism approach and there is truth in the Scientism approach and we make a tragic mistake when we take the attitude one or the other approach is The Sole Truth. As far as I can tell, the Bible says nothing about the mechanics involved in "Let there be light" and Astrophysics says nothing about the sentence as headline. The Logical Positivist may claim the sentence to be meaningless, but fails to realize it is a headline understanding of the Big Bang. While the sentence may be meaningless in matters of the mind, it is meaningful in matters of the heart and as I have yammered about elsewhere, we need both mind and heart to be complete humans.

—

Getting back to the idea of belief in -O- being a delusion. The delusion comes not in a belief in -O-, it is the belief in One Image of Him as Being Absolute Truth©. All images are equally incomplete when it comes to the Infinity; the best they can do is point to a Reality that is not describable. One way of thinking about these various images is they are allusions to a Deeper Reality. Belief in -O- is not delusional, as so many in the Scientism camp want us to think, it is allusional. The Source of all images is not an image in itself for the Finite can only point to the Infinite.

x>x>There is nothing in Science that says -O- does not exist; Science does not support some things that have been said about Him.
x>What is your take on all this?

I find it amusing that one of the initial goals of the Western Scientific enterprise was a presumption of 'Knowing the Universe to know God.' (Aquinas, I think.) The trouble now is the issue has been commandeered by radicals on both sides, turning it into something that is all surface and no substance. On one side, we have the Rationalist who claims that because Science rules out the Biblical image, all images are wrong while on the other we have Religionists who claim all images but the Biblical are wrong.

The fact that stars are not eternal says nothing about the Isness of -O- Himself. The Reality of -O- is not denied because Uncertainty says He may not be Omniscient. The critique calling -O- into question because the planetary orbits are not perfect circles is hubristic, what right do we have to question Him about Orbital Mechanics? Religion teaches us that -O- is one and Science teaches us that whatever is behind all this is one. I cannot make the jump to assuming the One of Religion is an altogether different One than that of Science and, as with all dualities, I cannot assume they are Competing Realities.

There is no conflict between the Rationalism inherent in the Scientific approach and the Intuitiveness inherent in the Spiritual approach other than radical hardheadedness - Science has produced reams of data that can be interpreted as what happened after He said "Let there be Light." The Creation and Eden stories of the Bible (As well as the stories of all Faiths.) are Statements of Gnowledge while the data supporting the Evolution of the Universe and Life are Statements of Knowledge. Within that which Knows and within that which Gnows lays a that which is beneath conception. Science explores that from one direction, Religion explores that from another angle, and neither, in and of themselves, is The Truth.

x>x>Much of this Theological wrangling can be solved by taking a new look at how we think about the concept of Oneness. The theory in the West is 'Oneness as Separate' while the East views it as 'Oneness as Manifoldness.' Both assert the Oneness of -O- by talking about it from different directions and this is where the misunderstanding arises.

x>I'm not sure I understand what you mean by misunderstanding.

We make a mistake when we think of Oneness in mathematical images and then apply it to Theological reasoning, for the One, by daffynition, must include the Many. -O- is Exclusive in that He is the Source of all images and Inclusive in that He is all images.

The problem we face is caused by assuming that Aristotelian Logic works as well in Theological discourse as it does in Scientific. In the same manner that an electron is neither a particle nor a wave exclusively, -O- is neither Exclusive nor Inclusive alone. -O- is not dualistic, our understanding of Him is, and this is entirely due to the dualistic nature of language. The West treats this issue as if 'If not the Biblical, then no God' both Theologically and Scientifically and both camps act as if this is a Truth that applies to the entire world. It is not the case that -O- is either this or that, for He is both and much more. The East treats this issue as 'Heaven' being beyond all this. One of the dualistic misunderstandings is thinking -O- is outside all this, which comes from a universal misunderstanding that -O- or The Divine is 'beyond'. Yes, He is 'outside' in that nothing in particular is -O- and yes He is 'Inside' in that He is the inside inside of everything in general.

The problem with thinking about the Oneness of -O- in Singular terms is that it limits the freedom of -O- to Be What He Will Be, as if we can force Him to fit one particular image. If the Singular is the -O-image of Christianity, the Singular cannot be the -O-image of Buddhism, according to this thinking. This Singularity school of thought leads to the spitting contests we all have about "Different -O-s" and "Which One is The Truth ©" which have nothing at all to do with -O- but our understanding of Him. Seeing as how it is fine for St. Paul to be all things to all men, it should be fine for -O- as well. No matter how our views of -O- differ, all I can say is that we have different -O-images, as -O- is the Source of the images, not any one Image in particular. To insist "-O- is this and Only this" is Idolatry and to couple this with "And you must believe it as well" is Blasphemy.

I know, I'm guilty of the skirting the edge of the former, I'm not guilty of the latter as I only claim this as my limited understanding. When I say "-O- is . . . ", I say "-O- is like . . . " with the idea that while -O- is Infinite, a -O-image is Finite. A -O-image is One while the Source is Many, for by daffynition, an 'Infinity' includes the One and the Many in a Reality that is more magical than we give it credit for being. I am not about converting others to my point of view as that is a decision best left between -O- and the individual. The most I hope to accomplish is to get people to agree to disagree on the issue of the Whatness of -O- as Universal Truth when the issues of Whatness are Relative Truths. -O- is one whatness to Jews, another to Muslims, another to Christians, yet another to Hindus, Buddhists, Confucianists, Taoists, and many other schools of thought.

Universal among these schools is the Isness of -O-. That we all believe should be of more importance than What we believe as far as I'm concerned. It matters not if one person likes Realism and another likes Abstract for they both like Art. As different as Pink Floyd and Benny Goodman may be, they both performed music. The most magical aspect of -O- is that as The Source of all images, He is large enough to encompass, and small enough to infuse, all images. Looking at the Whatness is looking at the outside while looking at the Isness is an inside point of view and both ideas, in and of themselves, are relative truths. The Ultimate Truth is there is noplace one can look and find -O- as well as noplace one can look and not find -O-. He is The Source of all things physical, all events mental, all that was, is, and will be.

Another universal concerns the Infinity of what by various names is called "God." I submit no one image can capture an Infinite as language is Finite, therefore not adequate to the task. This is not to deny that we need language to get our points across and to understand each other, just that language, like Newtonian Mechanics has a limit to its' effectiveness. Our image of an atom as a miniature solar system works up to a point just as our image of Humanity is neither male nor female. The problem is that Western Theology is still mired in Newtonian thinking on this issue, thus illustrating the Uncertainty Principle about the more one knows about God, the less one gnows about -O-. Just as an electron is neither particle nor wave, -O- is neither the Being of Western nor the Beingness, exclusively, of Eastern Theology as Infinity includes That Which Is as well as That Which Isnot.

It would be helpful to keep in mind that not only is 'The Name not the Thing', 'The Image is not the Reality'. There are times -O- feels like the Stern Father when He slaps me upside the head but that does not describe His Totality. It would be just as wrong to think of -O- as the Loving Mother who kisses the boo boos away and makes some hot chocolate. To some, He appears as A Being and to others, Beingness. At one and the same time He is the Source of both images thus neither image is Him. Just because He is The Ultimate Agent for Everything That Happens, this does not mean He has it all written out in a Grand Plan of Action. That mystical experience is called ecstatic does not necessarily mean that He Loves us in the sense that He has a Special Place in His Heart for Humans.

x>x>This Singularity school of thought leads to the spitting contests we all have about "Different -O-s" and "Which One is The Truth ©" which have nothing at all to do with -O- but our understanding of Him.

x>I have thought for a long time that you were condemning the 'various theologies', as you put it, but the more I read you, the more it looks as if you are taking them to task for what you said before was 'a profound lack of imagination' in their -O-image.

The various theologies put up these grand and glorious images, thinking they can limit the Isness of -O- to the Whatness of their image. Whatever -O- is in toto, is a Reality that cannot be put to words. I have long felt this mutual misunderstanding going on about the various Theologies, carried on mainly in the West, has caused more harm than good. I submit this harm will continue as long as we assume that we can apply scientific accuracy to theological discourse.

It is not the case the One and the Many are 'different realities', the case is they are different points of view of the same reality. Your image of -O- is outside and my image of -O- is inside and we both ignore that in/outside are complimentary rather than opposing; the One is completed by the Many, not lessened. Who are we to proclaim what -O- is In Totality? We give lie to the concept of -O- as Infinite when we assume we can describe -O- with less than an infinite amount of words and in less than an infinite amount of time. It would be an easier task to drink the Pacific Ocean with a fork or to swallow a red hot iron ball than it would be to totally map the territory.

It is also not the case, as so many are willing to assume, that if someone does not agree with the Biblical -O-image they are automatically Atheist. This is insulting to those who are followers of nonbiblical traditions, for one can agree with the concept of -O- and disagree with the Biblical image. Theism and Atheism are not the only stances as there is Nontheism as well. Theism postulates -O- as Being, Atheism postulates no -O- whatsoever, and Nontheism postulates -O- as Beingness. As far as I'm concerned, Atheism is nothing more than a rejection of the Biblical daffynition made under the misapplication of the logic that if there is no Biblical God, there is no -O- altogether.

x>x>The problem is that Western Theology is still mired in Newtonian thinking on this issue, thus illustrating the Uncertainty Principle about the more one knows about God, the less one gnows about -O-.

x>This almost sounds Agnostic.

It's somewhat a twist on Agnosticism, which I think of as Aknosticism. What is at question in this approach is not the existence of -O- but whether or not a human can know all there is to know about Him. I know beyond a shadow of a doubt that -O- exists, but I cannot prove it with the accuracy of $2 + 2 = 4$. I find it frustrating that I cannot find the words to give an adequate picture of my image, but I temper it with the recognition that -O- is a Reality That Cannot Be Totally Described. It saddens me that some take up their -O-image as literal truth, as if the menu was the meal and it aggravates me when they get into this 'True-False' silliness, for when it comes to the Totality, 'true' and 'false' are but linguistic conventions. If -O- were capable of being Totally Known, would that Reality really be -O- and why do we have to daffyfine -O- with Scientific Accuracy?

This is what saddens me so much about Western Theobabble, one assumes 'Different Images Describe Different Realities' along with 'One Image Is Truth And All Others Are False' as if they were Scientific Truths. If His existence is contingent on one true campfire story, it surely would make Him less magical than He appears in my mystical experiences. He does not tell me He is Not That, He tells me He is Not Just That. It is enough that He is. If He is, if one campfire story were true, capable of being Finitely Known, He cannot be the Infinite Reality that encompasses and infuses all campfire stories. -O- can be illustrated by light; He is neither Particle (Being) nor wave (Beingness) exclusively, and just as light comes in a full spectrum of colors, He has many faces and many names.

What saddens me the most is the attitude the 'Different Images are In Opposition' with each other for truth. Reality is not oppositional, linguistic blathering about it is. Just as my image of -O- as Beingness does not deny your image of -O- as Being, Particles do not deny Waves. Chinese is not a denial of Russian as a language, it is merely a different language. Each of us has some of the truth of -O- while none of us have The Truth©. The image of -O- as Being compliments the image of -O- as Beingness just as the northern compliments the southern pole of a magnet. The Images themselves may be opposing points of view but it is nothing more than two views of the same Reality.

I'm not looking to convert you to belief in a 'Different God' when I yap about my image, I'm pointing out, as I see it, the truly magical quality of imaging -O- as Infinite; that which is at the center of all images. Other than Isness there is no One quality that -O- 'has'; the Whatness we all yap about are aspects of Isness just as red is an aspect of white light and German is of cuisine. There is much more to -O- than we can put into any one image of Him, even mine of Him as The Source of All Images. The point I attempt to get across is 'The Image is Not The Reality', hoping to turn Idols into Icons, which is true theological thinking. While the Biblical daffynition of -O- is Iconic, the attitude that particular daffynition is the 'Truth For One And All' is Idolatrous as it is Belief in His Whatness rather than Faith in His Isness, putting Belief before Faith. When we share our images with each other, we are not saying -O- is that particular image, the sharing is a pointing at His Magnificence for He is All That and Much More. I can think of nothing as impressive that a Reality that is the Central Truth of All Things Great and Small.

x>x>I know my offering of "-O- is . . . " is an attempt at a Single Truth, but I am not offering more that a confession that -O- is, not an apologetic about what in particular -O- is.
x>I fail to see the difference.

The difference is that I will not reduce -O- to a single image that all must adhere to. At most, all I can say is "-O- is Infinite." - my image is as Incomplete as yours. I'm offering a thesaurus approach that acts as a Universal Translator that shows "faith" in Buddhism and "faith" in Christianity are different paths to the same goal. You discuss God from a Western point of view and I use Eastern phraseology but neither of us is speaking The Absolute Truth, for the words are but pale indicators. Holding the Image as Reality turns an Icon into an Idol and it has been written "Thou shalt not make unto thee any graven images." In the long run, there is no difference between a graven image of stone or wood and one of thought.
Some people have accused me of attempting to 'introduce a new God' into the fray, which is not what I'm attempting. All I'm doing is talking about a different way of conceiving the One, for we all admit that -O- is One and that -O- is Infinite. -O- is all images to all people and the Image is not the Reality, no matter how strongly we may believe in that Image. No matter how grand any one Image is, the nature of language is such that it falls short of The Glory that can be Gnown but not Known.

x>x>Why do we have to daffyfine -O- with Scientific Accuracy?
x>This question never occurred to me. Having come from a Biblical based religion, I have always assumed The Bible to be literal truth.

That is where I was when all this started. After a while, I realized there is Literal and there is Figurative Truth and it is my contention the Bible falls in the latter category. I'm not knocking the Bible here, I feel the same about all religious texts. Religious language cannot help but be figurative as it attempts to say the unsayable. As far as I have been able to discover, there are only two literal truths about -O- with the latter being an extension of the former. One is '-O- Is' and the other is '-O- Is Infinite'; anything else is commentary of figurative language. I realize this will sound strange to some people, but the less I Know about -O-, the Grander He becomes, for I have come to Gnow there is no aspect of Reality

36

He is not. As a kid, I embraced Christianity and found Him, as a youth I tried without success to ignore Him, as a young man, I studied many disciplines and kept finding Him under different guises, now as an old fart, I immerse myself in Gnowing 'It is enough That He Is.' I'm perfectly willing to let -O- Be what -O- will Be and not question why things are this way, as I know if I could question Him as to "Why?", His answer would be "Why Not?" Who are we to question why God appears to you and -O- to me when the Important thing is that He appears to both of us in a guise we both can somewhat understand? It does not shake my Faith one whit that you see God or that she sees the Goddess or he sees Allah, or he sees G-d., or that I see -O- as we are all seeing the same Reality, we just yap about it differently.

Literalism is a hindrance to Theology as it is a barrier to Interfaith dialogue and mutual understanding. There is one description of the Divine coming from the Gita, another from the Bible, another from the Qur'an, and so forth. These are figurative truths that help lead us to the literal truth of "-O- Is." An example of the problem of Literalism is the spat over evolution, for the figurative truth of the Biblical Creation Story is one campfire story and evolution is another about how all this came to be. When I talk about evolution, I talk about it as an ongoing event since the Big Bang; energy evolved into matter, some of it living. -O- 'created' all this, but I see Creation as an ongoing event rather than something that happened sometime in the past. It is like having a painting of the Sun on your widow. Faith in the Sun is expressed best by scraping the painting off the window to let the real Sun shine through. The painting is not the real thing; no matter how grand it is, it is still a figurative image. In the same manner, no matter how exalted a -O-image may be, it is a finite image of figurative language.

x>The peace that passes all understanding, Jesus said. This peace is available, though, without putting oneself as a part of God. The danger here, Dino, is that if we were to think thus, that our experience of oneness with God is, in reality, something that is us, rather than an aspect of God, we might begin to unconsciously think we are right in all our thoughts, or that we have divine rights to go with our shared divineness. No, to the Christian (and I think to the Jew, Muslim, and Baha'i also), God is a separate, holy Being from man, and man cannot ever attain a status wherein he is not different from God. God is wholly Other.

All I can do is speak from my experience. I know that -O- and I are one. The only divine right I have is to treat the -O- in others with as much respect as I treat the -O- in me. If -O- is the innermost reality of all of us, to treat anyone disrespectful is a sin. -O- is neither wholly Other nor wholly Self any more than the head and tail of a coin are wholly One or wholly Other.

—

This, and the few that follow were part of a discussion about the mystics' claim of oneness with -O-. There are too many people that automatically assume that a claim of Oneness is a claim of Identity - as if the mystic claiming Oneness is claiming Personal Identity. The mystical understanding of the Oneness of all does not allow for one having the experience to get fat headed about it, for the person next to me is just as one with -O- as I am. If I claim to BE -O-, then all it does is indicate how little I understand Oneness. (Besides, I wouldn't want the job.)

x>x>x>If there is a difference between my perspective and the Christian perspective, it is this; I do not believe Jesus was/is the only Incarnation of God. We are all God, just as Jesus is.
x>x>I understand your point, although I can't agree with the last sentence. I can see how, with your knowledge of eastern religions you might come to this conclusion, because, if I'm not mistaken, such unity is taught in eastern religion.
x>Not universally so. Hindu and Buddhist texts both refer to the 'uncreated, unmanifest, etc.' I am 'created' and 'manifest'. I am therefore not part of God.

The created and manifest is the physical body and the socially conditioned consciousness. The utmost center (The uncreated and unmanifest) of you is -O-. Too many people see dualistic explanations and assume the dichotomy is an Either/Or relationship. The relationship is not dichotomy, it is paradox - both sides of the issue are equally incomplete, in and of themselves. Without the 'uncreated' and 'unmanifest', there would be no 'created' and 'manifest', just like a battery must has both a positive and negative terminal for it to be complete. This is the paradox of -O-. I know that -O- is the most central reality there is and that the centermost reality of this silliness that goes by the name Dino is -O-. I know that the centermost reality of (insert your name here) is -O- as is the centermost reality of (insert the name of your best friend here) as is the centermost reality of (insert the name of your worst enemy here.)

x>x>x>Western brain whirling here, Dino. I can see what you mean, that God is in all things, and I agree with that -- in a way but to say that all things are God, to me, is to deny His sovereignty.
x>x>To the contrary, dear lady. It is affirming the Sovereignty of -O- to the highest. Without -O-, there would be nothing.
x>Maybe we're saying the same thing in a different way. No way could I ever think that I am God. I know me pretty well, and if I am, we're all in trouble.

I think the biggest issue here is the claim to be -O-. When I say that I am -O-, I am not claiming that I *personally* am -O-, but that the innermost reality of this reality called Dino is -O-. The innermost reality of you is -O- as well. Our innermost realities are the same reality even if we are separated by a generation, different sexes, and have had differing lives. This goes for each and every one of us simultaneously - and I know good and well I would rather not have this fool Dino to be in charge of the show.

What can be more Sovereign than the reality that is innermost reality of all? All too many misunderstand the mystic claim of "Oneness" to be a claim that they personally are -O- Incarnate; The Boss, in other words. This comes from imaging the human ego as a fundamental reality that is fundamentally separate from the fundamental reality we call -O-. The Oneness of the mystic is a radical Oneness that is Inclusive, not the Exclusive Oneness as popularly misunderstood although the former includes the latter.

Neohumanism

x>x>We need to recognize that if we existed in a different form, our concept of spiritual would be different as well for physical/spiritual is the same goeswith in the same seamless unity.

x>Are you discussing some form of Spiritual Materialism?

One of the greatest mistakes I find in Philosophy and Theology is this constant dissing of physicality, a pessimistic approach that I find degrading. What these people fail to recognize is the glass is half full with physicality and half full with spirituality. As far as I'm concerned, we give insult to -O- by degrading physicality, for as I keep yammering, if it wasn't for physicality as we misunderstand it, spirituality would not exist as we misunderstand it.

This Western idea of a conflict between -O- and Satan that somehow ended up 'tainting' the physical world coupled with this 'temptation' story to explain death shows a profound lack of Theological Imagination. My answer to the Eastern ideas that physicality is a burden that 'must be overcome' is that 'I cried because I had no shoes until I met a man who had no feet.' Physicality is not a hindrance to Enlightenment; it is part and parcel of it. Physicality may be random at the lower levels but patterns emerge from the randomness and these patterns have significance. We need to realize the Physical is just as important as the Spiritual for Life is not an either/or type of situation. As with all dualisms, Life is Spiritual/Material, not Spiritual and Material in some form of parallel coexistence.

Humans are the universe come alive and aware, a point these people who deride the concept of evolution by saying we 'devolved from monkeys' miss. Of course, it isn't helped by "The Descent of Man", which is a wrong-headed look at it as far as I'm concerned. Our stage as monkey-like critters was but a short period of time in our rise from the basic energy of the universe, which is but one of the manifold expressions of -O-. Rather than being part-time visitors, we are part and parcel of the whole shebang. If the Earth is an example of how the rest of the Universe does its business, there must be a huge amount of life out there. No matter where we look on this planet, there are living organisms, and to conclude life arose on this one planet alone is absurd, but for now let us discuss life on Earth. From the sheer number of living organisms on this planet, one could come to the conclusion that one of the functions of the planet is to produce life. When I use the term 'functions', I'm not talking about a mechanical process as if it were some factory spitting out widgets. This is something the Earth does of itself, like a flower being a way for a seed to make more seeds.

One thing we must keep in mind that it does not matter if we are discussing the smallest semi living virus or the largest organism, each have one thing in common, if one can call life a 'thing', but you get my point. A dead whale and a dead virus have the same physical components as the other half of the story but there is a vital something missing that is common to both. Life can be manifested as a bacterium just as it can as a human and we are constantly finding new examples of life in extreme environments. It is absurd to think this something we call life in a human is somehow other than this something we call life in a rabbit. Yes there are differences between being a rabbit and being a human but the point is they are both living beings, sharing that something vital with each other and the aforementioned whale and virus. What is this something we all have in common?

The physical aspect of our existence is one commonality. Both a human and a virus are composed of physical matter and that physical matter is composed of patterns of something we cannot daffyfine. The mental aspect of our human existence is one commonality as well. The human soul is a pattern of something we cannot daffyfine either. I submit that if two somethings are equally unknown, it is safe to assume they are but aspects of the same something. That something in one human is the same something that is in another human. If our 'soul' is a totally unique and eternally existing reality, there are some awkward questions to ask. One is 'where were we prior to our existence?' For years I have tried to think of something along the lines of a huge storage locker where our souls are stored until it is our time to play in the sun. This would require another storage locker for those who have come in out of the rain and I cannot see that being the case, given that recycling seems to be the universal order of the day.

We are right in saying each human is unique, but we are wrong in assuming said uniqueness is eternal and total. That hidden self mentioned above is the same something I labeled the centermost reality elsewhere in this discussion. It seems that -O- enjoys physical existence and the mystical experience is rightly called 'Ecstatic', although I would prefer a term like 'Ecdynamic' for the experience is far from static. Despite the fact the experience contains common features, it never is the same twice in a row, each building on others.

I have no idea why -O- chose physical existence in a human body (at least here on Earth), but I will not despair over His choice for to do so is sacrilegious. Your complaint (About death being inevitable.) reminds me of a painting I read about once, referring to three gentlemen with three reactions to tasting vinegar - one complained that it tasted sour, one complained that it tasted bitter, and one said

—

it tasted like vinegar, just like it is supposed to. As it is said somewhere in Taoist texts - Heaven went through all this trouble to give you a body and you yap about 'hard and white.' This is why I disagree with the goals of eternal Heavenly existence and eternal Nirvanic nonexistence; one approach runs away because vinegar is not honey and the other approach runs away because of the bad taste vinegar leaves in one's mouth. Both approaches completely miss the point that vinegar is supposed to taste like vinegar, not like wine or a candy bar.

Yes, there is pain and suffering entailed with physical existence and yes, life is temporary. Be that as it may, have you really considered what it would be like to be alive forever (supposing for the sake of the argument that we have eliminated all forms of suffering and the effects of aging.)? I don't care how beautiful they are, sunsets must get boring after the first thousand billion. We both like a nice steak dinner, but I wonder how long we could stand it as a steady diet. Eventually one would learn everything there is to learn and then one would run out of surprises. I prefer to live in a reality wherein I can follow a curve in the path that leads to a face to face with a dragon.

One of my downfalls in College was that I kept finding interesting classes that were not directly related to the degree I was after, taking them for the sheer joy of learning something new. My ex-wife used to complain that I was moving on because I got bored, but it wasn't like that - I just kept on finding pretty pebbles in the sand. Many of my professors used to tell me that if I weren't careful, I would end up becoming a professional student. This spilled over into my life after I left college, where I have pretty much drifted from job to job through Temp Agencies. Everywhere I went, I found interesting aspects to the job, pretty pebbles on the banks of the river as it were, and that enthusiasm for learning new things has led me to become a 'professional temp'.

The point of the above little aside is that if one wishes to consider each new field of study or job a new life, it is somewhat analogous to the Cycle of Life and Death. -O- keeps coming back to learn and experience new things in a never-ending cycle where He does it in all places at the same time. Just as nutrients are recycled in the physical to fertilize new growth, mentrients are recycled in the spiritual/mental to fertilize new growth. A Tree may only live for a certain amount of time but the Orchard continues just as a Human lives for a certain amount of time but Humanity continues. We are, in a manner of speaking, going against the will of -O- by the running away to an Eternity Somewhere Else.

We need not despair for all this is -O- and whatever happens will happen. Rather than mope about temporality, consider that eternity only lasts the lifetime of a single individual while the Eternal continues. There is no point in complaining about change when change is what spurs growth and keeps everything new. It does not matter that you personally will not receive your Reward for doing good in the afterlife because afterlife and beforelife are merely relative to the Eternal Now. One makes a mistake in assuming that meaning must come from an outside agency in the same manner that 'law' implies 'lawgiver'. The fact of randomness as a central 'working' of the quantum level of reality does not mean that life has no purpose, for like 'meaning', 'purpose' comes from within. Likewise, we need not run from a natural course of events just because we do not like certain aspects of it. It seems like the business of Reality is to make more points of view of itself. As the saying is misquoted - 'The eyes are the windows of Reality.' and as we all know, a person can look in a window as well as out. It seems to me that we commit sacrilege with our attitude about existence; we condemn and run away from that which we should be celebrating. -O- becomes aware through each human being . . . One way to describe it is that -O- sees through our eyes, hears through our ears, speaks through our mouths, and so forth, to continue the above quote beyond talking about Earth. This does not mean that I'm advocating traditional hedonism - "Eat, drink, and be merry, for tomorrow we die." Doing so would be going to the other extreme, which is just as much a mistake. As I've been saying all along, life is a balance and it is only rare cases where one extreme or the other is in control. We need to treat the physical aspect of life with the respect it deserves, no more and no less. Sister Mind needs Brother Ass just as much as Brother Ass needs Sister Mind for we cannot have one without the other. Neither hedonism nor asceticism carried to extreme can be done to the glory of -O-. As Jesus pointed out, one must eat in order to be able to observe the Law, but, if one is stuffed to the point of lethargy, one cannot observe the Law either.

x>x> Somehow we fail to realize that it is through the physical that the spiritual becomes evident.
x>I'm not sure what you are trying to say here.

My complaint about most traditions is what I see as a lack of perspective when it comes to Brother Ass. For whatever reason, it has turned out that here on Earth, Mind/Body goeswith in a seamless unity that extends from the 'smallest' subatomic particle to the Universe as a whole. It does us no good to complain about the changeability and temporary nature of physicality, as it would not change the facts of existence as we know them. We miss the point when we degrade Brother Ass because sometimes he lets us down; just because some men do evil things, that does not mean that all men will do evil things. The opposite is true as well in that although some people are saintly, not all are, so Sister Mind sometimes lets us down. By concentrating on the extremes, we ignore the means and the overwhelming majority of people are decent folks, despite the rascality in each of us.

In our confusion over Mind/Body or Spiritual/Material, we have a tendency to lean towards the 'side' of Mind and Spiritual and tolerate the other 'side' as little as possible. The sides only exist linguistically - 'brain' and 'mind' are two ways of talking about the same reality. As I have talked about elsewhere, in a dualism, we cannot have one without other. Take one 'side' away and the other 'side' will vanish as well - modify one, the other modifies in response; consider what it would be like if all the bees in the world were to suddenly vanish. We need to recognize that if we existed in a different form, our concept of spiritual would be different as well for physical/spiritual is the same goeswith in the same seamless unity. We further compound the error when we conceive of the individual human soul or ego as central to our existence and this is because we are confused over the concept of individual. As far as I have been able to tell, there is only one reality that fits the daffynition of 'individual' and that is the totality we choose by various names to call -O- and that is the Centermost Reality of all.

It makes absolutely no sense to degrade Brother Ass because it does exactly what it is supposed to. We might as well treat the vessel -O- has come up with to become aware through the perspective of Earth with the respect it deserves. In a manner of speaking, it is just as blasphemous to disrespect physicality as it is to disrespect spirituality, as both are of the selfsame unity. I have this odd feeling that if I could ask -O- Why? concerning physicality, His answer would be Why Not? This is why I contend the two traditional approaches are mistaken, for the universe "peoples", trees "apple", and although a person or a tree dies, Humanity, Orchards, and Life go on in a constant state of change. Hoping for eternal existence in Heaven denies Life from one extreme while hoping for eternal nonexistence in Nirvana denies it from another. It is the eternal part of both equations that is one aspect of the mistake, for nothing except -O- is eternal. All Reality, Physical and Mental, is compounded and as the Buddha said, "All compounded things are subject to dissolution." Another aspect of the mistake is the assumption that Heaven and Nirvana are realities somewhere else, while the truth of the matter is that Heaven is a glance over the right shoulder while Nirvana is a glance over the left.

There is no reason to assume that we can get off the Wheel just because we do not enjoy the cost of the ticket. We can work together to make the situation here on Earth less painful. We can join together to eliminate terrorism. If we put our minds to it, we can eliminate hunger throughout the world. Monetary motives need not be the primary drive for the Pharmaceutical Industry's distribution of medicines. We can work to ease conflict no matter where it may arise. We can work to achieve true equality between all humans in all phases of life. Yes there are situations that make me sad. But to let those things overshadow the joy that can also be found in life is to miss the point entirely. All along I have been talking about balance and this applies here as well. Sometimes life is wonderful and sometimes it is a pain in the ass, sorta like a wobbling top that refuses to fall over.

I'm not suggesting we go to the other extreme and make an Idol out of Physicality, for Human Life is a balance between the Spiritual and Physical Realms. Just as Awareness is the Spiritual aspect of -O-, Body is the Physical aspect and is therefore just as Holy, deserving the same respect. We do great disrespect to -O- when we denigrate the vessel He has chosen because it does not measure up to our standards. Physicality is not evil, not a burden to bear, not a result of blind, random interaction, not something we are trapped in, not a hindrance to Enlightenment and death is the natural result of Life. Celebrating our physicality does not mean we can throw off all moral guidelines and behave in any manner we wish; one can enjoy food without being a glutton and wine without becoming a drunk, in other words. If one hangs exclusively in the Spiritual, one misses the beauty to be found in the Physical and remaining solely in the Physical eventually becomes a cheap thrill. It is not the case that we should take one extreme or the other in our philosophy of life for balance is a function of Reality. One cannot contemplate the Glory of -O- when one is either sleeping off a huge meal or feeling the effects of self-punishment.

There is a middle approach between asceticism and hedonism and while the extremes can lead to enlightenment, they tend to be a hindrance as they become paths unto themselves. To control the desires by eliminating them is just as a wrongheaded approach as is giving in to them without a struggle. Sexual desire is not a problem, for example, behavior based on sexual desire is - there is a major difference between looking at a beautiful person in appreciation of the beauty and leering in lust. For most of us, it is not so much what we eat that leads to health problems, it is how much of the bad stuff we eat. On occasion, a fast food burger is not a problem.

x>x>Side comment - all too many Westerners confuse the 'I am -O-' idea of the East to mean 'I personally am God.' . . . . "Thou Art That" is ignored for the attack on the "self-centeredness" of Eastern Religion.
x>What do you mean?

Realizing the -O-head within oneself is only part of Eastern Theology. Another part is the realization of the selfsame -O-head within the other person. Although the Enlightenment Experience is unique for each person, it is not a unique experience in and of itself, limited to one person. We all share the Divine in equal proportions for -O- is no respecter of persons, 'making' each of us an Icon of The Most Holy - the Unenlightened and the Saint each are emanations of the Divine.

You see, I may be -O-, but as -O- is not noOne, but Everyone, I am not -O- and the same holds true for you. From the extreme of 'outside' -O- 'contains' me and from the extreme of 'inside' I 'contain' -O- as do you. 'Outside' and 'Inside' are relative terms for the selfsame Reality. It is absurd to assume the 'inside of you' is a different Reality than the 'inside of me' for it is the One selfsame Centermost Reality given voice through the Many. Look at classical music for example, while a violin is an important part of the Orchestra, there is a need for the Oboe as well as the cymbal. The Music itself is not a quality of any one performer, but a harmonious blend of all performers in point and counterpoint. Paraphrasing what I quoted earlier, -O- pretends to be you so successfully He forgets He is also pretending to be me. I submit "Each of us is an Icon of the Divine" and "We were created in God's Image" are two ways of saying the same thing. Elsewhere I've yapped about looking at it is if humans were 'sense organs' for -O- for when the -O-head in me looks into your eyes it sees the -O-head in you looking back.

I think much of the confusion is due to stopping at the Enlightenment experience rather than continuing to what the results of Enlightenment are. Enlightenment is the end of the means of the mystical path, but Enlightenment is a means to further ends. Another part of the confusion is based on the difference in thinking of 'individual' in the West and the East. The Easterner does not consider the 'individual' as a totally separate and eternal being, taking the attitude 'I and only I am personally God Almighty' as meaningless to the enlightened person, for a self-centered approach is contradictory to the essence of Eastern teaching on this issue.

x>x> . . . death is the natural result of Life.
x>That certainly places you in great odds with Christianity, which teaches that death is the result of Original Sin.

That campfire story is degrading as far as I'm concerned. Some tell the story that it all can be traced to Eve eating the apple in the Garden; evidently before that, there were to be just Two Immortal Humans on the planet. Does anyone telling this story ever stop to consider how others view it? For example, what significance does the Eve story have to a person who has a religious worldview that does not include Biblical Eden Imagery? If you don't believe in Biblical Creation, you certainly are not going to believe that you are going to die because of something your supposedly long removed ancestress did. When a tuna dies, what does the Eve Story have to do with it? I fail to see how Original Sin leads to the death of a redwood tree or an earthworm.

Nothing in Reality is Eternal with the exception of the basic energy that is central to all and the only constant there is change. It has been shown over and over that the Universe recycles energy; with the recognition that humans are part and parcel of the whole shebang, death becomes a minor issue. This is not to say the act of dying is of little concern; I would much rather die in my sleep than be victim of a drive by shooting, for example. Like I said earlier, Eternal Life in the physical realm scares me as eventually the Newness of Reality vanishes. I'm scared of the idea of Eternal Nonlife as it misses the point that life and consciousness are essential processes of the Universe.

As far as I'm concerned, the main reason for our fear of death is that we fail to recognize who we are as well. We have this campfire story about how we are temporary visitors and not of this world. The story is told that our relationship with -O- is, at most, that of an adopted child, which is far from the case. We are Living Icons of The Most Holy; -O- is The Central Reality of physicality as well as consciousness. It is one and the same Central Reality in my physicality as the same Central Reality in my consciousness as it is in yours and all other sentient beings. Why get all freaked out about all that time after death but not all that time before birth?

Neoepistemology

x>x>x>In what way is Theory and Theology the same?
x>x>Theories are incomplete answers in Science and Theologies are incomplete answers in Religion.
x>I hadn't considered it quite this way before, but I think it works.

What I am discussing by 'incompleteness' is the failure, in the ultimate sense, of either a theory or a theology to completely describe Ultimate Truth. Spiritual Reality is more than can be encompassed by any one Theology just as Physical Reality is more than any one Physical Theory. I submit the so-called dichotomy between science and religion is the result of rhetoric by fanatics on both sides of the issue - each side has been too busy clubbing each other with Dictionaries to bother looking at a Thesaurus. The radical materialists have their image of Reality, the radical religionists have their image - one side is looking at the head of the coin and the other side is looking at the tail.

I find it quite amazing that people can argue seriously about the Ontological status of theoretical terms in the philosophy of science. We have no right to sit back and claim, "There ain't no such animal", and simply on the reason the present level of technology prevents observation. The history of science is resplendent with examples in which theory becomes fact, which I feel should be enough warning against denying any possibilities.

Whether the terms under discussion have been "Crobes", "Mesons", or "Warm", it seems to me that we constantly treat knowledge not only as cumulative, but complete. One example of this is the argument that translight velocities are impossible because Relativity says so. At one time in human history, it was considered impossible for people to fly or to travel faster than 60 miles per hour. Not only can we fly in space but also we can reach speeds of 300+ MPH in a quarter mile drag race. It seems to me that people take the limit of a theory as a barrier to further knowledge rather than a goal to surpass unlike they do with physical speed limits.

How proud science was in the late 1800's when the claim was made that all science had left to do was to fill in the blanks! It is humbling to admit that perhaps we do not know as much as we think we do and that we may be creating the very entities we are looking for, as one line of thought in Quantum Mechanics considers possible. When we assign the dividing line between Theory and Observation with the intention of keeping the barrier in place permanently, we automatically limit our viewpoint by excluding other possibilities, ones that may be just as valid in their context.

Using the terms "Theoretical" and "Observational" is to me, a continuance of the habit of reductionism so fashionable in the West. It is like the other dichotomies prevalent in Western Philosophy; as Hegel (I think) pointed out, "They muddy the water so that they appear deep." Take, for example, the split between the known and the unknown, treated in the West as each gain in the former as a loss in the latter. If the charge of Hubris deserved, this is where it would rest. Only since Quantum Mechanics sunk in has the folly of this attitude become somewhat obvious. The impression I get from the various disciplines I have studied is that of kids standing in a back lot yelling, "My Daddy (School of thought) can beat up yours!" Philosophers in general are so adamant that the leaf is indeed red the rest of the tree suffers from neglect. I fail to understand how people can honestly argue against a method a basically meaningless expulsion of modulated air is used, for all definitions are incomplete, in and of themselves.

There is nothing sacred about any phrase we use, for language is the medium humans utilize to arrange experience in a somewhat comprehensive manner. What difference does it make whether it is a Zen Master or a Sociologist that refers to the majority of people as 'Sleepwalkers', the message is still the same. To insist that a term or phrase is theoretical and therefore meaningless is slapping a rather stale picture on the universe. Even the great Einstein was not immune from dogmatically based ridicule over the Theory of Relativity. Look at the situation, Einstein was suggesting that what we have been assuming was flat is curved and that time itself is relative to the observer. The concept of Relativity was treated as nonsense by many of the leading scientists of the day. But of course, they had an interest in maintaining the status quo of their school of thought. The major hindrance is in not looking at the term 'nonsense' in the frame of 'Not available to common/rational sense'. It seems to me that studying the history of any discipline will show that contexts change in some peculiar manners at times with the total message remaining becoming more significant.

When we try to comprehend the implications of a nonsensical statement with 'normal' Aristotelian logic, it is like attempting to grasp water in one's fist; all we end up with is a wet hand. No matter how strongly we wish to believe in our version of the truth, it must eventually be realized that sidestepping the issue does not prevent the bull from sneaking in a side door, catching us by surprise. When one has the bull by the horns, the thing to do is to jump on its' back and enjoy the ride. Either/Or logic, like Newtonian Mechanics, has its own context, in which it is the most appropriate explanation we have. Our trouble lies, in part, from the habit of taking meanings from one context and attempting to apply it to another context. The problem with concentrating on the red leaf is a tendency to trip over something on the ground, or to miss the forest for the leaves. When I think about the various schools of thought, I get the impression of horses with blinders on, all traveling the same path, all thinking they are alone, that they have the best and smoothest route.

There is one manner of viewing the ontological significance of the dichotomy between Theoretical and Observational entities, and that is as a psychological goal for the increase of scientific knowledge. We can use the terms Known and Unknown rather than Theoretical and Observational. After all, the term Theoretical is usually reserved for terms that are unknown at the time they are introduced and many turn out to be Observational and even may reach the level of 'common sense' knowledge. If we must insist on a real change in physical status, at what point can we say the neutrino is real - does it gain existence with the disintegration of nucleus, or with discovery in particle accelerators, or with the theory's conception? Perhaps the neutrino became 'Real' after a certain 'critical mass' of scientists accepted the theory.

By careful reading of the history of science one can see that much of what was unknown at one time is now known. I am not going to make the foolish claim that at some time, all will be known and that science will come to an end. The more we come to know, the more we come to realize that we do not know that much after all. We will never run out of questions to put before Nature, even if it is a version of 'What is around the next corner?' Quantum Mechanics investigates two aspects of energy; that which is in the context of particles and one in the context of waves, each of which is a partial picture of the whole event. This implies there is more than one answer to a question in any discipline.

One would think the success of reductionism would show to the most casual observer the silliness of calling any concept meaningless. If one decided to, every event in the universe could be reduced to a single reality, making a rational argument in the process. A good argument for Determinism can be put forward, as can an argument for Indeterminism in Quantum Mechanics, Theology, and Psychology, among other fields. Many things that we accept today WERE completely unbelievable at one time in the past. We are always coming across this. There have been authoritative pronouncements that no one would reach the moon because of incontrovertible evidence of one kind or another. At one time it was believed that if a person traveled far enough in one direction, they would fall off the edge of the world because, as we all knew, the world was flat. There is really no sense in considering many terms 'observational'. Take the term 'Warm', for example, it means one thing to my lady friend, another to me, and yet something else to a Tibetan. The term 'Red' has no ontological significance to someone who has been blind from birth. Mass is Mass, whether one is discussing it from a Newtonian context or an Einstienian one.

x>x>In some ways, this resonates with the Eastern Christian (And one that is quite strong in the Franciscan voice in Western Christianity) about the inability to speak of God or rather the inadequacy of anything we could say about God. God's transcendence is such that we can behold him as much as our substance will allow, but our current state is such that 'anything said of God is inadequate for the very reason it can be said.' There is an absolute truth, but language fails miserably.
x>Maybe. I'm not convinced language per se has been given a thorough trial. (Certainly most 'natural' languages have failed, but that's a separate issue.) Do you believe that the truth cannot be known? And if known, do you believe that it should not be shared or proclaimed?

The truth is the reality beneath the words, not the words themselves. Yes, we all should share our mutual incompleteness. My incomplete understanding is different than your incomplete understanding and I hope that I will never be so foolish as to take my incomplete understanding and use it as a club to beat up on your incomplete understanding. (I'll get into a 'My -O- is smaller than yours.' discussion but not the other way around.)
Look at what is going on in this conference - people from both sides of the various spitting contests are throwing out insults - we have people in here who make a profession out of showing how all branches of Christianity are false except theirs - we have a constantly growing cult list - the discussion about Evolution has devolved into an Either/Or shouting match - things non Christian are interpreted as anti Christian - religions that do not ascribe to the uniqueness of Jesus have been labeled false - we have an argument going over the 'proper' method of Biblical scholarship - we have a person throwing out cheap shots against Eastern mysticism based on obvious ignorance about Eastern mysticism.
What is all this fighting over, anyway? The argument with Mormonism is nothing more than a disagreement over Theological interpretation and is really no different than the difference in interpretation between Jewish and Christian Scriptures on the Nature of -O-. The argument about Evolution is all about a literal interpretation of the Bible and it is hard to tell the extremists of either side apart. What is this ever-growing cult list but someone's rather restricted interpretation of what it means to be Christian and in some cases, a religion at all?
Look at what the arguments are attempting to say - 'This and only this is the truth and all other opinions are wrong.' We drown in the Sea of Spirituality

when we cling to our faith as a rock when faith is in actuality our water wings. There is an old Zen story about how this nun had a golden Buddha, and to make sure it got plenty of sweet smelling incense, she had a funnel placed under the Buddha's nose. Soon the Buddha had a dirty, black nose. How is this nun's behavior any different from the behavior of someone who insists there is only one correct understanding?

Creation is a golden Buddha - Creationism is a black nosed Buddha. Likewise, Evolution is a golden Buddha - Evolutionism is a black nosed Buddha. Taking the Bible as literal makes it a black nosed Buddha. Using Creedal differences to beat up on each other devolves Christianity into a black nosed Buddha. Arguing over the method of Baptism makes Baptism a black nosed Buddha. All the arguing over whether or not the bread and wine actually become the Blood and Body turns Communion into a black nosed Buddha. What has the clinging to a belief in a complete truth accomplished in the long run but strife?

-O- is a living Reality, not the NT, the Book of Mormon, the Qur'an, the Tao Te Ching, the Dammapadma, the Gita, the Torah, etc. This is not to say that they are false, merely equally incomplete understandings, as is the materialistic understanding. I fail to comprehend how we can all admit that -O- is infinite, then turn around and insist there is only one proper understanding. Am I the only one who sees a logical absurdity in this? Those who place their Book on a pedestal would do well to heed the admonition of reading the Scriptures and thinking they have found life. -O- is not found in, but through Scripture, no matter which Scripture we are talking about.

I suggest the outcome of this clinging has led to what can only be described as Idolatry.

Idol-a-try
1: the worship of a physical object as a god.
2: immoderate attachment or devotion to something.
Websters' Dictionary

I am using daffynition #2, as it is my opinion that #1 is too restricted - it should include our mental images, for they are no less idols than those carved from wood or printed on paper. The idea that there is a 'Complete Truth' is an example of this. How can the infinite be limited to one daffynition? Each daffynition, in and of itself, is incomplete and the truth is much grander than all our silly spoutings put together.

x>x>How is this nun's behavior any different from the behavior of someone who insists there is only one correct understanding?

x>I appreciate the imagery of the golden and black nosed Buddhas, but the premise of your illustration is prebiased. Your assumption is that there is no complete truth, while the Christian faith holds that our Scripture is the revealed Word of God. Whether or not you choose to accept the Bible as God's revelation is neither here nor there, but to require Christians to accept the world's religions as equally valid alternatives is to require them to stop being Christians. I'm not interested in beating anyone up with my beliefs; however, I don't wish to be told that I must relinquish them for the common good either. It does not please me to give offense, but the funny thing about the truth is that it must exclude error.

All I ask is for is that you understand my position and I promise not to try to convert you. If you wish to consider me an unrepentant pagan heretic who is doomed to Hell, that is fine with me. You can even tell me these things in a polite message. When you try to make it the Law of the land, you are overstepping your bounds. (I am using 'you' in the generic here.)

x>x>-O- is a living Reality, not . . . This is not to say that they are false, merely equally incomplete understandings, as is the materialistic understanding.
x>You argue your points well, however, you have dismissed at the outset the possibility of the revelation of objective truth. If God has said in the Bible that there is only one proper understanding, then the logical absurdity would be to deny it and to choose to believe something else.

To me, the logical absurdity is restricting -O-'s Word to the Bible. I find the train of thought that -O- spoke to humanity only through the Bible to smack of Spiritual Pride.

x>x>Religion without Science is blind, Science without Religion is uninspiring.
x>I'm not sure what you are getting at here. Are you saying we need both Religion and Science?

Having Religion without Science goes too far in one direction and having Science without Religion goes too far in the other. Religion concerns our Intuitive and Science concerns our Rational aspects, and when we deny one aspect of ourselves, we become less Human. It is my contention the so-called dichotomy between Science and Religion in the West is the result of radicals on both sides of the issue getting caught in the trap of Dualistic thinking. The way most Westerners view it is that Religion and Science are in an antagonistic relationship where one attempts to disprove the other and claim to be the Temple of Truth.

When most Westerners think "Religion", they are thinking Bibleism, and when they think of "Science," they are thinking Scienceism, because that is how they are taught to think of it. This does not have to be the case for Bibleism is not the entirety of Religious thought and Scienceism is not the entirety of Nonbiblical thought. This is where the proponents of Scientism fail; they make the unwarranted jump from disproving Geocentric Astronomy, for example, to assuming the nonexistence of -O-. The only thing Science has 'Proven' is that some Western theological concepts are not supported by what we have learned. Likewise, the proponents of Bibleism make the mistake of claiming the Bible to be Literal, Historical, and The Source of Truth In All Matters©. The only thing Bibleism has 'Proven' is that it is but one of many ways to express Religion.

Science, in general, and Religion, in general, has nothing to fear from each other for they are not antagonists. We make a major mistake when we assume the truth lies in Scienceism or Bibleism exclusively. Science is an expression of the Rational aspect of Humanity as a whole. Religion is an expression of the Intuitive aspect of Humanity as a whole. Humanity is neither Totally Rational nor is it Totally Intuitive and we do ourselves a disservice when we limit ourselves to one mode of thinking over another. In the Western part of the world, there is a Science based philosophy of Nature and there is a Religious based philosophy of Nature, each having their strengths and weaknesses.

The universe, according to Western Religious Tradition, is an Artifact constructed by a separate and outside entity, with all the parts following laws imposed by said entity. At the 'end' of Creation, the universe was pronounced "Good", but there was a rebellion in Heaven, evidently in a fit of spite, Satan caused the universe to be tainted with evil. Humans are 'fallen' creatures, and each of us is tainted with 'Original Sin', which is the result of Satan successfully tempting Eve into eating forbidden fruit. Scienceism kept the machine image of the universe and the creatureness of humans while throwing out the Divine.

Not all Religions and Philosophies see things in that light. Images of the universe in the East are organic rather than mechanical. Common to all Eastern Faiths is the idea that -O- is neither 'separate' nor 'outside.' The concept of 'Original Sin' is nowhere to be found in any of the Eastern Religions for death is natural and not the result of Divine Punishment. The whole idea of Satan as a being working to counter -O- as a being cannot be found in Hinduism for -O- is not viewed as a being. Not all Religions have the image of Humans as 'fallen creatures', finding the imagery to be appalling and undignified. At the worst, we are wayward beings who have forgotten who we really are, and at the best, Humans partake equally in the Divine Nature. In Buddhism, all people are capable of obtaining enlightenment. Taoists and Confucianists believe that any person can become a sage.

There are many forms of the answer that we are Material Beings, that mind is the result of a peculiar arrangement of said matter, and said mind dissipates with the death of the body. On the other side of the coin, we have variations of the idea that we are Mental/Spiritual beings where the body is the result of the mind, with said mind going to another level with the death of the body. Each side contains a bit of the truth but I submit neither side alone has The Truth©. What we fail to take into account is that this is not an Either/Or situation for Body and Mind are but aspects of the same . . . shoot, I cannot think of a name for it. The problem with both approaches is that they fail to see that without the one side, we would not have the other side for balance.

Without body, as we misunderstand it, we would not have mind, as we misunderstand it. It is a mistake to assume that because mind and body are different types of reality, they are fundamentally separate realities. Likewise, it is a mistake to assume that because both undergo change, they are false, for they each carry a pattern that continues and the pattern is real. These views are neither true nor false in the Absolute sense, merely incomplete because we have a tendency to overlook the idea of Relationship. The relationship is not mind or body, it is not mind and body; it is mind/body, much like the relationship between certain flowers and certain bees.

x>x>I have never been able to accept the theory that nature is an Artifact and that the soul is something tacked on from the outside or the theory that that nature is Mechanical and that mind is merely the byproduct of brain activity.
x>What other options are there?

On the one side, we have Evolution*ism* and on the other we have Creation*ism*, or the new name, Intelligent Design. The trouble is that members of each side of this issue act as if they speak for everyone. What these people do not realize that one can adhere to the concept of Evolution without thinking it is accidental and to the concept of Creation without attributing it to Biblical understanding.

The Creationism argument depends on Biblical Literalness, Bibleism. All cultures have a Creation Myth that can be included in the Intelligent Design concept. Hindu Theology has a story that is just as good an example of 'Intelligent Design' as Biblical Creation is; yet I would be willing to bet this fact will never be acknowledged by the proponents of Intelligent Design. The Evolutionism argument is based on a mistaken assumption that if there is no Biblical God, there is no -O-. Hindu theology talks about the soul evolving from the lower animals, but the idea of a link between Western and Eastern thought, as talked about in such books as "The Tao of Physics" caused a minor uproar in those who ascribe to a Scientism worldview.

My complaint about Creationism is the story that it is an event that can only be explained by a Literal and Historical interpretation of the Christian Bible. The Biblical story of Creation is a good allegory of what may have happened, but that does not mean It Happened That Way. A major problem with Bibleism is that the Bible never does explain where Cain and Abel got their wives. If, as it is said in the Bible, Adam and Eve were the only humans that were propagating, the wives of the sons were their sisters and that means Humanity is the product of incest. Another problem with Creationism is that it takes the story of the Tower of Babel to explain away the differences in various groups of humans. In this story we hear that -O- is concerned that we are getting too smart for our own good; He scrambled our languages and I'm going to assume this is where our genetic differences arose also. What the proponents of Bibleism are saying is that German, French, and American English have been around and unaltered since the fall of the Tower.

My complaint about Evolutionism is that in the drive to separate Science from Religion, Scientism arose as a nonbiblical religious theory that refutes the validity of other nonbiblical religious theories along with Biblical religious theory. A major problem with Scientism is that it doesn't take the Religious aspect of life as sincerely as it should, passing it off as 'metaphysical' or 'mythical' because it isn't 'factual.' One reason for this attitude is that for most of its history, Scientism has dealt with Religion as if Bibleism were the entirety of Religious experience.

It does not follow that if some Western theological concepts are shown to be mistaken that all theological concepts are mistaken and the same holds true for the other direction. The beauty of the concept of creation is that -O- is, the universe and all in it is not the result of mere accident, and there is a Reality greater than all this. The beauty of the concept of evolution is that if one starts the story at the moment of the Big Bang, we see that (at least here on Earth) energy evolved into Living Sentient Beings that can sit around and discuss the possibilities of how it may have happened. The mistake of Bibleism and of Scientism is the claim that one and only one of these stances is the Sole Arbitrator of Truth.

One of the arguments used by those who promote Intelligent Design is but the latest variation of the 'A Watch implies A Watchmaker" reasoning. There is much truth in the story but assuming two separate entities having nothing in common with each other makes a mistake. Transliterated (loosely) into Eastern thought, the Watch is the Watchmaker. This intelligence is not something that is Other, it is the floodlight referred to earlier; the awareness that underlies Awareness. I like to think of this as -O- playing Hider - Seeker in which -O- Hides in the physical (Yang) and Seeks in the spiritual (Yin) aspects of a deeper unknown Reality (Tao).

The Universe as Machine image that has been so successful in Western Scientism depends on the validity of Newtonian Mechanics as the Sole Truth. As a worldview, it is a contrast to the image of Universe As Organism and one is just as mistaken as the other. What we have been finding lately is that the parts do not follow the same rules the machines do. Under the Newtonian Mechanical Universe is the Quantum Organic Universe wherein causality does not seem to be a factor and how things look depends on how we choose to look.

The image of Humans as biological machines, controlled either by genetics or environment, is giving way to an image that transcends Either/Or thinking. Our relationship with the universe is not an accident of Nature for the machine is not dead matter; Energy evolved into Matter, Matter evolved into Life, Life evolved into awareness, awareness evolved into Consciousness. Looking at it from a Science point of view, we are the universe come alive and looking at it from a Religion point of view, we are the 'Mind' and 'Body' of -O-.

x>I have been attempting to get what you are trying to say for some time now, but I am still a bit confused. For all your talk about Incompleteness, you do not deny the reality of either side. The best I can come up with is that you are a Monist, but how can that be if you affirm the reality of both sides of the Dualism?

There is a difference between Classical Monism and Neomonism in that in the Classic Monist Stance, one side of the dualism is subjected to the process of reductionism to prove the validity of one side and the falsity of the other. What I'm talking about can be called Radical Monism in that 'each side' is as 'real' as 'the other'. What I am talking about is not Monism, as much as it may appear on the surface. My stance is a radical nondualism in that both sides of the picture are equally real, in and of themselves, yet neither side is the whole picture.

Perhaps the main difference between the Classical Monist stance and that of Neomoism is how the solution to the existence of the Dualism is approached in the first place. In the Classical approach to the Mind/Body Problem, for example, the Mind Only people would have us believe that it is the Consciousness/Soul that is Ultimately Real while the other side would have us believe that Mind is simply a lucky arrangement of matter. Proponents of each side claim that the evidence of the other side is "Illusions", with the connotation of being "Fake" being understood by the majority.

On the other hand, the Neomonist approach acknowledges the reality of both sides of the issue in a limited sense. The problem with understanding this approach is the majority of people discussing the issue use the term "Illusion" as well in their talks, which I feel is a mistake that helps continue the misunderstanding. By substituting the term "Allusion", we are not injecting the connotation of "Fake" into the imagery by taking the phenomena as Symbols of a Deeper Truth.

Each side of the issue is relative truth, but is not the whole truth of the issue; the Truth is more than both sides. Without Body, as we misunderstand it, we would not have Mind, as we misunderstand it, and by the same token, without Mind, the question of Body would not come up.

While the substitution of terms may appear to be a minor nit-pick, it leads to a major difference in the way the issue is approached. Rather than falsifying the sides as the term "Illusion" implies, the sides are relatively validated with the use of the term "Allusion". This substitution also moves us away from our normal Either/Or pattern of logic to an area where the Either/Or aspect of the issue becomes meaningless.

x>x>The Neomonist approach acknowledges the reality of both sides of the issue in a limited sense . . . Each side of the issue is relative truth, but is not the whole truth of the issue; the Truth is more than both sides . . . Rather than falsifying the sides as the term "Illusion" implies, the sides are relatively validated with the use of the term "Allusion".

x>Are you saying there is no way to escape the Paradox that is involved in what we call Reality?

Yes I am. The answer to the problem of Dualism is that we are asking the questions in the wrong manner, and one reason for this is the Logical System the West has had forced upon it. I am not saying that Aristotelian Logic is useless, what I am saying is that it should not be used beyond its legitimate boundaries. We cannot state with authority that it is either Nature Or Nurture that molds our personality – the Truth of the issue is somewhere between the extremes. It is my contention that our desire for absolute certainty is the major reason behind these hassles, for in the long run, absolute certainty is a contradiction in terms.

x>x>All theologies/theories are equally incomplete.

x>I really feel rather sorry for someone like you who places so little trust or confidence in his own belief system, to repeatedly call it, as well as all others, "incomplete".

I have utmost trust and confidence in my belief system. I am not going to be silly enough to claim that because it works for me, it must be what everyone else must believe or be doomed to Hell. As for calling it "incomplete", it is. I am only human after all, how in the heck could I have full knowledge of the infinite? It seems to me that you are misunderstanding "incomplete" in the context I am using it. Newtonian Mechanics is an incomplete understanding in and of itself of the physical world - that does not mean I have no less respect for it than I do Quantum Mechanics, which in itself is an incomplete understanding. The fact I call the theologies incomplete in no way demeans -O-. It is, IMHO, an affirmation of the highest order. -O- is much grander than anything we humans can imagine. That you restrict your image of -O- is saddening from my POV for it seems to me that you are restricting -O-'s ability to BE. When one focuses on a particular aspect of Infinity and claims that small portion is the whole truth, one commits Idolatry. Once one takes that image and uses it to hold oneself as superior over another, the line has been crossed and the sin of pride is added to the sin of Idolatry.

I have so much faith in -O- that I do not need to stand on the street corner and call attention to myself or to my theology. I do not have a -O- given ministry to pull others away from the faith they feel is right for them. My faith is so strong that I can honestly say that you and I are equally loved by -O- and I would consider it an honor if you would let me buy you a cappuccino at St. Pete's Bar and Grille. I'll make you a deal, you give me a tour of the City and in return, I will give you a tour of the Countryside.

Neoethics

x>What I fail to understand is that if there is no personal reincarnation, thus no Karmic retribution or reward, and without the promise of Heaven or the threat of Hell, what does it matter to me in the long run to behave ethically during this lifetime?

Neomonism offers a new view of our relationship with ('with' is really the wrong word to use, but at present I cannot think of a better one.) the Universe. Given that the dichotomies of Mind/Matter, Spiritual/Material, and -O-/Man are allusions to a Deeper Truth, the point is that we are the Universe become alive and -O- become Aware. This requires a new look at what it means to be human and believe it or not, comes with its own set of Moral Imperatives. Bottom line is that although I know down to my toes that -O- and I are one, I don't have the right to run roughshod over others, who are just as equally one with -O-.

To teach that each of us is an Icon of -O- and then to turn around and treat that Icon with less than utmost respect is sacrilegious and shows to me the person involved in such behavior does not understand the meaning of enlightenment. Although one might get caught up in the sense of Power that comes with Enlightenment, it is just a passing phase of the experience, which is replaced with a profound sense of Humility. There have been plenty of times that I have wondered what I have done to deserve such a rare and terrible gift. Having said all this, I can attempt to answer your question, but I will start somewhat in the middle and more than likely take a bit of a roundabout wandering answer.

Let us look at this Heaven/Hell/Eternity thingie first. The whole thing makes absolutely no sense with a theology that includes the ideas of Cyclic Time rather than Eternity and Change rather than Stagnation. No matter how hard I attempt to accomplish the feat, I cannot equate whatever it is I call -O- with the idea of Eternal Reward in Heaven or Eternal Punishment in Hell. To hold to an idea that -O- would condemn someone to Eternal punishment is to show a profound lack of trust in -O- as far as I am concerned, for -O- is not into Self-abuse. I highly doubt if the idea of all those people sitting at the foot of the Throne and staring at the Holy Presence for all Eternity is -O-'s idea of a fun day either, for eternal pleasure is no different than eternal pain. I submit that people have a sideways view when they think of Eternal as 'Days without end', as if time goes on forever and a day somewhen back in history and will relentlessly march on forever and a day somewhen in the future.

This view of time as a straight arrow is not the only view, for in the East, time and the universe are seen as cyclic; more along the lines of 'what goes around, comes around.' type of thingie. Yes, there is overwhelming evidence that time does indeed flow in a straight line, but that is at the macroscopic level, but that is not always the case at the submicroscopic level. On the physical level, time, as we understand it begins to make its effects felt at the microscopic level. We can no longer assume that time goes by at a constant rate throughout the universe, for Relativity Theory shows us that the experience of time depends on the speed the observer is traveling relative to the event being observed. The image of time as an Entity that flows in one direction from forever in the Past to forever in the Future does not coincide with the universe, as we understand it so far. We find too many cycles in Nature to assume that time has immunity from the same process.

Along with that thought, it is rather silly to assume the universe itself is immune from the recycling process as well - the Big Bang happened to start this chain of events, what is to say that this is the only time it has happened or will happen? With cyclic time, the concept of eternal Reward/Punishment makes absolutely no sense. It also calls me to question you about your meaning of the phrase 'in the long run' for, like the relativity of Time itself, what is considered long term by one may be a brief moment to another. A Morning Glory sees but one while a Redwood may see hundreds of thousands, yet to them, the passage of time seems equal.

From a psychological point of view there is no such animal as an eternal stimulus for if something is constant, it blends into the background. If one stays on a constant high from a drug, eventually the high feels like normal life, causing one to need more of the drug to maintain the high in a never-ending battle. The constant Reward of Heaven or the constant Punishment of Hell falls in the same line of thinking - after a few trillion years, -O- would have to raise the level of the stimulus so that one could recognize that one is either being Rewarded or Punished. In other words, Heaven would have to become a better place and Hell would have to become much worse if the Promise or Threat is to be kept, and we cannot have that as Eternal is supposed to be unchanging.

I used to have a major issue with the way -O- was portrayed in the different churches I went to as a youth. My maternal grandparents attended a Presbyterian Church where the minister concentrated on the Loving aspect of -O-. My mother sent us kids to a Southern Baptist Church where the minister showed a preference to the -O- who Condemned Sinners to The Eternal Fire. My parents got divorced when I was about seven and I do not remember anything about church before then. For a while, we lived close enough that I would ride my

—

bicycle over to my grandparents to spend Sunday with them, which included going to church. While the -O-image talked about by the minister was strict, He was not Vengeful in His Punishment - the parables of The Prodigal Son and Good Shepherd was used frequently.

We eventually moved too far away for me to attend Church with my grandparents and I started going to a Church my Mom picked out for us. (When I think back, I wonder if the reason she picked that particular Church was that it was close.) It was a shock to hear about the Jealous and Vengeful -O- talked about by this minister and it was this dichotomy that started me on this mystical path. The major thrust of his sermons was -O- striking down His Enemies and their resultant Eternal Punishment. The next summer, I found myself going to Vacation Bible School where the central theme was the Holy Army of -O- based on a blend of the Crusades and the Knights of the Round Table.

No matter how hard I tried, I could not image -O- with the Bloody Robes, Eyes like Fire, and Tongue like a Sword. It was the song "Onward Christian Soldier" that caused me to take my first step on the path; like Kirk in one of the Star Trek movies, I had to question why -O- needed an Army. The second step was in questioning why -O- would be Angry at someone He had to Condemn to Hell because He created him or her to behave in the manner that caused his or her Condemnation in the first place. I was out walking around one day trying to get around this image of -O- as a Warrior King when I had the second or third mystical experience, this one generating what can only be described as a sense of utter revulsion and the thought of 'This is not Me.', which quickly changed into a feeling of being utterly Loved and Accepted simply for being me.

Granted, these were not the conclusions I came to as an untutored preteen, those came much later in life. Nothing I have experienced along this path has come even close to the idea that Eternal Punishment in Hell is a possibility. This is not to say that -O- does not punish us when we mess up, just that our Punishment fits the Crime - one does not get a Life Sentence for smoking pot. I could never accept the idea that -O- gave us but this one short chance to get it all right and then move on to some sort of Eternal Existence. Every time -O- punishes me for screwing something up, it is always a temporary affair and when I'm done doing time, I am once again a productive member of society. To me it feels more like the being put on restriction by a stern Father than being sent to Prison by a strict Judge.

Yes, I know, I'm talking about -O- as if He does exist as the Biblical -O-. As I discuss elsewhere, there are times when one has no choice but to talk as if that were a Truth. There is no difference in this than in talking about subatomic particles as if they exist as real things in and of themselves or yapping about the Ego as if that Ghost were real. The -O-image I'm using is Hindu in that I see punishment as the working off of negative Karma in this illustration - once the Karmic debt is repaid, the soul is back on the journey to reunion with -O-, which brings us to another part of your question.

Until now, I have been yapping as if I believe in the idea that the central aspect of Humans and -O- are separate entities and that humans have an Eternal soul, while from my outlook, there is only one soul going through all this and that is what you would call the Holy Ghost aspect of -O-. To misparaphrase Hinduism, -O- is acting out all the parts at the same time with such skill that He never realizes what He is Doing. What good would it do for -O- to Reward Himself with Eternal Bliss when Bliss is a Central Truth about that which by one form or another, we call -O-? On the other hand, could he come up with a Punishment that would make Him Suffer for All Eternity? In either case, it is sorta like asking if He can make a rock so big that He cannot lift it.

While Karma may not attach from one particular human life to another particular individual in Panentheism, there is no denying the existence of something like the sins of the fathers being visited on the sons. There are people that exploit others and people that are exploited by others in a strange yet sensible balance. Things that happened generations ago come back to haunt us with almost regular frequency and it seems like we always attempt to replace one extreme with another which does nothing more than add fuel to the fire. Poverty is a problem because nobody (Generic) has done anything serious about it - we all know that American farmers could feed the world if American business wasn't so greedy. We still have disease simply because we have yet to figure out how to defeat them, but we are working on it. The main reason for Racial Tension is that in the past, European Whites went around nailing lifts on the natives' feet in a sincere but misguided effort to make the world a better place for themselves and their descendents.

As far as I'm concerned, this idea of Personal Karma is a reality much like the ego and the wavicle - things that must be in order for the world to make sense. It does make sense to explain that someone exists on the edge of malnourishment because in an earlier life they were a glutton, but it is merely the surface of the story. The Central Truth is that because gluttony has existed in the past, malnourishment exists today, and the judgment of Karma is not an indicator of personal guilt, but the guilt of humanity as a whole. Because Karma is impersonal, it does not matter who in particular suffers, just that a balance is maintained, for like it is said in the Bible, -O- causes it to rain on the Just and Unjust alike. To sorta repeat what I have rambled about elsewhere, the story of the Individual Soul is a myth, as is the story of Individual Karma.

So, to finally get around to answering your question, it matters how you behave because we are causing harm in both directions when we behave less than ethically. Take slavery, for example. By holding another person in this state, you are harming that person by the conditions of their life and you are harming yourself by acting like a jerk. As I have discussed elsewhere, one factor of human history has been our search for freedom and only in rare examples are there free slaves. When you enslave someone, you are denying the -O-head within him or her and denying him or her the ability to be what they want to be. By being a slaveholder, you are degrading the -O-head in yourself by ignoring that the two of you share the same Central Core Reality and at the same time are two of many facets in the Divine Jewel.

Enlightenment brings certain responsibilities with it, foremost being that your behavior is a direct indicator of the depth of your understanding. One cannot say, "Thou art -O-." and use that person as a means to an end at the same time while claiming to be Spiritually honest. By the same token, one cannot realize the -O-head within and take it to mean that one is The Boss, with all the perks that come with it. In one respect, the yak about Enlightenment being 'liberating' is true, but in another, Enlightenment is a 'restricting' experience as well in that although you are completely free, there are certain things you cannot see yourself doing. This is analogous to what Christianity talks about with the tale of Law being written upon ones' heart, although the immanent aspect of -O- writes this Law.

Let us take the Law against Murder as an example and define 'Murder' as the unjustifiable killing of a human being. From my point of view, the Law is redundant in that I cannot foresee myself taking that action. I can think of instances where the killing of another could be justifiable, but for the moment I am discussing the general situation, not a special one. The Law written on my heart, as it were, is more than adequate to prevent me from offing someone for the heck of it and I know myself well enough that I would bring down more punishment on myself than the Penal System could. I do realize there are some of us who do require the Outside Law to keep them from committing murder, but I honestly feel they are the vast minority when contrasted to Humanity as a whole.

x>I'd like to explore something that you have got me thinking about. You mentioned that the idea of "Christian ethics" or "Christian morals" made you a bit uneasy.

x>I have a personal view that ethics and morality are universal, and are probably reflected in the belief systems of each society. If we put a 'moral person' from each of those faiths in a room with a 'moral person' from the eastern religions, how much common ground would we find?

I am uneasy about the attachment of the label "Christian" to morals as it has a tendency to cause others to think they can only be found in Christianity.

Hopefully you realize that I would feel the same if the daffyfiner "Taoist" was used as well.

Eastern religions teach not to lie.
Eastern religions teach not to steal.
Eastern religions teach not to murder.
Eastern religions teach respect for all humans.
Eastern religions have a Golden Rule.

Of course, people who follow Eastern religions are not perfect, but none of us are. If you set aside the theological differences, we all have pretty much the same ideas about how we should work together.

"Do unto other as you would have them do unto you."
"Do not do to others what you would not want done to you."
Although both statements above lead to people treating each other better, I have seen hotly defended philosophical discussion on the relative merits of each. The former is usually held up by some as 'better' than the latter statement, simply because it is a proactive statement. I fail to see the difference between treating another respectfully because that is how you wish to be treated and not treating another disrespectfully because you do not wish to be treated disrespectfully. When you do not treat with disrespect, you are actively treating them with respect, or at worst, are neutral to them.

There is no Religion that I know of that says murder, theft, lying, illicit sexual behavior, cheating, and related behaviors are acceptable. Is the person who refuses to steal because of Christian morality really any different from a person who refuses to steal because of Buddhist morality? There is no discernible difference between the Jewish concept of honoring your mother and father and the Confucian concept of respecting one's elders. A Taoist is just as likely to stop and help a person in trouble as a Baha'i is. If neither a Muslim nor a Hindu child cheat on a test, does that make one better than the other?

In the long run, all of us are saying the same things; we just have different ways of expressing these concepts. The religious structure called Christianity is made up of the same bricks and mortar the religious structure called Hinduism is, as is the structure called Buddhism, the one called Islam, the one called Taoism, the one called Baha'i . . . Each of these structures may appear to be alien, but they are only different styles of architecture. A Mosque is alien to a Temple as a log cabin is alien to a gingerbread cottage. There are many mansions in my Father's House . . . to me this indicates that -O- has a place for each of us. It makes sense to me that if Jesus had meant there was only one mansion in His

Father's House, He would have said something along the lines of 'There is a mansion in My Father's House which I go to prepare.'

The common understanding of "one" is one in mind or accord, which is but a surface reading of what Jesus was saying. I do not think Jesus meant anything other than complete nonduality (a compound unity) when He discussed the Oneness of -O-. This nonduality is not any different than the nonduality of Ramakrishna, Lao Tzu, Buddha, Nagarjuna, and other sages of the East.

Faith in -O- is the diet of the Spiritual life and in the vision of clean and unclean foods, -O- was showing Peter that all Spiritual food is clean. It does not matter to -O- if we partake of the fish of Christianity, the ox of Judaism, the lamb of Hinduism, the rice of Buddhism, or whatever sustenance He has provided a person. I fail to understand how people can fail to see the universality in this vision, both within Christianity and within all religion. What matters to -O- is not so much how we worship, the crux of the matter is that we worship. When one accords himself with the Tao, one is doing the same thing as following Torah. Following a particular school of thought in Buddhism is, in essence, no different than following a certain denomination in Christianity.

x>x>I do this not because I have to . . . because I want to, out of the respect for the -O-head in each of us.

x>Is this an aspect of something we talked about a long time ago that you jokingly called Panencarnation? What does Panencarnation do for the idea of responsibility for our behavior?

Yes, I know the term panencarnation started out as a humorous play on the term Panentheism, but the more I think about it, the more accurate the term becomes. With panencarnation, one does not have to dive into the silly issue of Personal Karma as an explanation for why bad things happen. I know this is a paradoxical point of view - the individual is an allusion, yet it is the individual that influences events. There is no individual to generate bad Karma, yet individuals suffer the effects of it. Rather than Personal Karma as an explanation, panencarnation involves what could be labeled Apersonal Karma - what someone sows, someone reaps.

That someone suffers from the effects of poverty does not mean that they were rich at another's expense in a previous life, what it means that someone caused suffering and someone suffers. On the other side of the equation, someone doing good will result in someone receiving good. In other words, we suffer not for what we did individually, but what we do as a whole and we rejoice not in what we do individually, but in what we do together. In the short run, we each are responsible to each other for what we do in this lifetime and in the long run, we are responsible to future generations for the quality of life we leave them

(This is the Ongoing Judgment; the quality of life we experience is the Ongoing Judgment of past generations.)

If I act in a hateful manner in this life, not only am I responsible to those who I mistreat, I am responsible to those who may suffer from being mistreated in the future as I will be creating a karmic situation where someone will suffer from being treated in a hateful manner. On the other hand, if I act in a compassionate manner, I will be setting up a Karmic situation where someone will benefit from compassionate actions, both in the present and in the future. Ultimately we are responsible to ourselves to be the best human beings we can be, as we have to look ourselves in the mirror each morning plus we have to consider the legacy we leave our descendants.

That we are all Avatars is a given in Panencarnation, with a different understanding of the concept. My rewriting of the definition of Avatar:

Avatar

-O- becomes incarnate in many places at the same time through avatars (Icons of -O-), while -O- remains entirely full.

Unlike the Traditional Hindu understanding of Avatar, we fully participate in Human suffering and in becoming Human, like how in the successively smaller pieces of the hologram; we lose the resolution of our connection with the Divine. The idea of the Avatar and the idea that each of us is an Icon of -O- are essentially the same idea.

Panencarnation offers a new view of our relationship with the Universe. Given that the dichotomies of Mind/Matter, Spiritual/Material, and -O-/Man are allusions to a Deeper Truth, the point is made that we are the Universe becoming alive and -O- becoming Aware. Contrary to what we have been taught, we are neither outside visitors, nor are we the result of an accidental combination of random events. Just as visible light is an integral part within the phenomenon we call the Electromagnetic Spectrum, we are an integral part within the entire realm of things. -O- hears through our ears, sees through our eyes; each of us are the sense organs of -O-, in other words.

The Ultimate Paradox

x>x>Yin may be the opposite of Yang as Intuition may be opposite of Logic, but the opposition is complimentary rather that confrontational.
x>That is a contradiction.

Is the contradiction in reality or in our understanding of reality?
"Survey says",
Paradox can be defined as that which appears to be a contradiction, but is not. If there is substantial evidence in support of both sides of the supposed contradiction, then we can say that it is a paradox. If something is demonstrably real, then it can't be a contradiction.
My comment,
It has been demonstrated that light is a particle and it has been demonstrated that light is a wave.
"Survey says",
If one finds a questionable assumption at the core of the seeming conflict between the two assertions, then the contradiction is suspect, and the burden of evidence shifts to the other side. If someone produces a logically or alogically consistent resolution of the paradox, then it's either a paradox, or at least, a hypothetical paradox. Contradiction has been ruled out.
My comment,
The assumption that light [ANYTHING] is one or the other is questionable.

The answer to the problem of Western Dualism is that we are asking the questions in the wrong manner. I am not saying that Either/Or thinking is useless, what I am saying is that it should not be used beyond its legitimate boundaries. Where the problem lies is the attitude that Ultimate Reality is either one of the extremes, which leads to Reductionism, which as far as I am concerned, is a highly unbalanced way of looking at things.
The First problem with Western Dualism is that it is automatically assumed that each side of the Duality is a fundamentally separate and distinct entity. That which is Material is not Ideal, in other words. The Second problem is that it is automatically assumed that one must be reduced to the other. We miss the point

entirely when we assume that Reality is entirely explainable in either Material or Ideal terminology for Reality is more than either. As I see it, more attention has been paid to which side of the duality is the Whole Truth than to what is the Truth Of the Whole.

This gives rise to Monism; the idea that one side of the Dualist Equation is Real while the other side is a byproduct. One version of Monism would have us believe that everything in the Universe can be reduced to, and explained in, Materialist terms. A competing theory is that all things are byproducts of mental activity. Then there is the mind-stuff compromise wherein mind and matter are but reflections of each other. The mind-stuff compromise comes the closest, but one change is needed – they are not aspects of each other, but aspects of something else. A female is not an aspect of a Male and a Male is not an aspect of a Female, but of Humanity, in other words. Particles are not aspects of waves and waves are not aspects of particles, both are aspects of the basic energy of the Universe. You see, in the process of explaining the Parts, the Whole has been ignored.

What I find amazing is that typical Monism completely ignores the idea of "Oneness". As typically understood in the West, the concept is taken in the context of 'exclusive'. This is not the only understanding of the concept of "Oneness", for it can also be taken in the context of 'inclusive'. In the East, one side of the "Oneness" is viewed as an 'illusion', which is no different than the Western approach. One aspect of Reality is Material and one aspect of Reality is Ideal; the Totality is neither Material nor Ideal. Reality is a dynamic balance between the Yang of Materialism and the Yin of Idealism.

The problem with viewing reality as being composed of two separate entities is that we cannot understand how one element can affect the other. Reducing one element to another is a partial answer for no matter what, 'both sides' of the issue remain with "Yes, but . . . " questions. No matter how gracefully mind is reduced to matter or the other way around, the simple fact remains that whatever this Reality is, if it is going to be "One", it must include both Material and Ideal. But it is not a Reality that "has" both Material and Ideal Elements, but a Reality that exhibits both Material and Ideal behaviors. It is the idea of 'Separate' that is at the root of the problem, for this is a questionable assumption. It is like the so-called Wave/Particle Duality, each is not a separate reality but a behavior of the same reality looked at differently.

Although I am advocating a Monist solution, it is unlike traditional monism in that I am not denying the reality or denying the importance of either side of the dualistic equation. The universe is a balance between Material and Ideal and would be quite different if one or the other were missing. In the Game of Black and White, it is through our senses the world becomes sensible. What I propose is that we look at dualism not as an Either/Or duality but as a Flower/Bee unity.

x>x>Then again, one has to question the assumption of separateness, for there is really no separation between the environment and the mind.
x>Could you explain this a bit, please?

Look at what goes on in the case of vision, for example. Photons emanating from the sun travel through space, then the atmosphere, striking a surface and knocking off other photons that travel through the air, through the eyes, which translate them into electrical signals. Then they move up the optic nerve, through the synapses of the brain, which turn them into electrochemical signals that are somehow translated into vision. Then there is all that is involved in causing the resultant light to appear red. Where can we place a line to indicate where the event called 'body' ends and the event called 'mind' begins? There are two translations of energy involved, one at the eyes and one at the synapses. It is just as correct to say 'mind' begins with the translation at the eyes as it is to say that it begins at the synaptic translation.
The same type of stuff goes on when it comes to our sense of hearing.

Sound waves are carried through the external auditory canal to the eardrum, causing it to vibrate. These vibrations are communicated by the ossicular chain in the middle ear through the oval window to the fluid in the inner ear. The movement of the endolymph stimulates in the cochlea a set of fine hairlike projections called hair cells . . . The hair cells transmit signals directly to the auditory nerve, which carries information to the brain. The overall pattern of response of the hair cells to vibrations of the endolymph encodes information about sound in a way that is interpretable by the brain's auditory centers.
Microsoft Encarta 2000

Does hearing happen in the mind alone or is it a continuum of events from airwave pressure to eardrum movement to synaptic response?
Along the same example that the sunset would not be red without eyes, without ears, a falling tree makes no sound. No matter where we look, we find that we are intimately interconnected with the surrounding environments. The image of Separateness is in need of questioning, much in the same manner that Quantum Theory called Newtonian Theory into question.

x>x>What I propose is that we look at dualism not as an Either/Or duality but as a Flower/Bee unity.

---

x>Let me see if I understand this correctly – when one looks at the parts, it is a duality, but when one looks at the Totality, it is a unity. It also seems, from other things you have said, that you prefer an Organic to a Mechanistic view.

Yeppers. It is like the question of the nature of light; if we are looking for particles, that is what we find and if we are looking for waves, that is what we find. Further into the nature of light, we find both particle and wave in the same [whatever] through the Compton Effect. What we fail to take into account is that neither Particle nor Wave is the Thing in Itself, which is what is under discussion.

I have never been fond of the Watch and Watchmaker imagery as it just is too simplistic a view to be worthy of whatever it is that is -O-. The universe is too full of mystery and surprise to be considered a well-designed machine. One can take apart and reassemble a machine, which is something that cannot be accomplished with the universe. A much better image, in my warped view, anyway, is that of the Flower/Bee arrangement in which Flowers represent the Material and Bees representing the Ideal.

The Mechanistic Image of the universe is but a partial view as far as I am concerned, for it is nothing more than a surface scan. Yes, when one looks at the universe from the thinking of Reality as consisting of separate parts, the image of a Wonderful Mechanism is there. The deeper one looks, however, one finds a subtle interplay of the 'separate' 'parts' with influences spreading in all directions. Each 'part' of the Flower depends on the other 'parts' for its' existence while at the same time, the 'other' 'parts' require its' existence for their existence.

An Organic Image fits better with what we have learned about Reality than does the Mechanistic Image for one simple reason. The Mechanistic Image has the Mechanic on the Outside – The Watch and Watchmaker Myth. What is being found through Quantum Theory is that 'Control' is generated from within – Material Reality is 'built' from the quantum level up, to greatly oversimplify things, just as flowers grow from the Inside Out.

x>x>I do not think we should hold Either as Final Authority, they should balance each other in a seamless unity with the whole ball of wax being a *re*presentation of That Which Is.

x>Why use "*re*presentation" when what you are talking about is an image of "That Which Is."

That is because I'm not talking about coming up with an image, for The Ultimate is utterly beneath being portrayed in a single image. We cannot say it is Material

—

alone and we cannot say it is Ideal alone. One problem I see with images is that once one has an image of something, it becomes resistant to change.

The other problem I have is that the images become more important than what they are imaging. What we are doing is fighting over whether Positive or Negative is predominant when the subject under discussion is battery. The problem in yapping about what a battery is entails the 'and', for it implies duality, just like a single coin may have a heads and a tails 'side'. Somehow, we got fascinated with the behaviors and quit talking about the 'thing in itself'.

x>x>What I find amazing is that typical Monism completely ignores the idea of "Oneness". As typically understood in the West, the concept is taken in the context of 'exclusive'. This is not the only understanding of the concept of "Oneness", for it can also be taken in the context of 'inclusive'.

x>I'm not sure I understand the difference between 'exclusive' and 'inclusive' when it comes to "Oneness"

The headline story is that 'exclusive' is singular while 'inclusive' is manifold. As discussed in the thread called "Radical Agnosticism", Traditional dualistic thought holds that Ideal is exclusively Ideal and Material is exclusively Material. As I have been attempting to say about dualism, the problem is that it is assumed there are 'two separate realities'. Traditional Monism picks one 'side' of the issue to be the exclusive truth and reduces the other 'side' to the state of illusion. The problem with the monistic answer is that it is an incomplete look at the situation.

On the other hand, the Radical Nondualist (Or Radical Monist, from another point of view.) approach acknowledges the reality of both sides of the issue in a limited sense. The problem with understanding this approach is the majority of people discussing the issue use the term "Illusion" in their talks, which I feel is a mistake that helps continue the misunderstanding. By substituting the term "Allusion", we are not injecting the connotation of "Fake" into the imagery as we are taking the phenomena as Symbols of a Deeper Truth. Each 'side' of the issue is relative truth, but is not the whole truth of the issue; the Truth is more than both 'sides'. Without Body, as we understand it, we would not have Mind, as we understand it. I hope you do not mind if I borrow a bit from the thread we are in entitled "Panencarnation", but it fits in with what we are presently talking about. There is a Transcendent and an Immanent aspect to -O- just as there is an Ideal and a Material aspect to Reality. -O- is neither Transcendent nor Immanent exclusively, and Reality is neither Ideal nor Material exclusively.

In a manner of speaking, one can consider the Ideal 'side' of reality as Transcendent and the Material as Immanent. Although I keep using the term 'sides' in talking about dualisms, it is like the sides of a coin in that we cannot have one without the other. I think the hindrance to the whole issue of dualism is that when we image a duality, we image a dividing line between the extremes of the issue. This line is looked at as a barrier that prevents each side of the equation from interacting with the other side. It is the idea of barrier that gives rise to problem of Interaction, for what we envision as a barrier is actually a porous membrane that acts like a filter. Using a line as an image gives one a static view of Reality when Reality is actually dynamic. We can turn our mental vision 'sideways' and see that a line is a circle on its' edge.

I think this is the reason I rely on the Yin Yang symbol of Taoism as a symbol of my thinking. One neat quality of the Yin Yang symbol is the impression of dynamic motion and another is that each 'side' has a bit of its' opposite within. The black area can be imaged as the Material aspect of Reality with the white *re*presenting the Ideal. Reality itself can be imaged as the entire symbol. One has to admit there would be something missing if either 'side' of the symbol were missing.

x>x>The problem with the monistic answer is that it is an incomplete look at the situation.

x>What you are saying, in essence, that this is it and that is it, yet neither one, nor both, are It. There is no way around it, so one just accepts the paradox?

What I'm attempting to point out is that the paradox is only there when one tries Knowing the Universe as the only source of Truth about the Universe. It is our over reliance on Logic that is the problem, for Logic can only take us so far. Once we reach the limitations of the Logical Process, we need to jump from Knowledge to Gnowledge, where the paradox is seen as a moot point. Another cause of the paradox is how we think about the area of Metaphysics.

The term metaphysics is believed to have originated in Rome about 70 BC, with the Greek Peripatetic philosopher Andronicus of Rhodes (flourished 1st century BC) in his edition of the works of Aristotle. In the arrangement of Aristotle's works by Andronicus, the treatise originally called First Philosophy, or Theology, followed the treatise Physics. Hence, the First Philosophy came to be known as meta (ta) physica, or "following (the) Physics," later shortened to Metaphysics.
Microsoft Encarta 2000

This gives us the impression that Metaphysics is something beyond Physics when in actuality, Metaphysics concerns what is within Physics. A Metaphysical Truth is an Inner Truth while a Physical Truth is an Outer Truth. The Outer Truth of Electromagnetic Radiation is there are Particles and there are Waves when we look and the Inner Truth of Electromagnetic Radiation is there are wavicles when we are not looking.

Wavicles are not something attached to the outside of the Wave/Particle duality but an attempt at understanding the inside to the dualism. By searching for Metaphysical Truth 'outside', we confuse ourselves and end up acting like a puppy chasing its tail. The Outer Truth is that there is a Physical and a Mental aspect to our lives. The Inner Truth is that 'both' aspects are a single unified reality much like the positive and negative poles of a battery. On the outside it seems as if each of us is a totally unique individual, but we all have more in common than we do in difference. Each of us may have differing personalities, but beneath the ego, we are all 'part' of the same Reality, Avatars, as it were.

By focusing outward at the parts, we get lost in the nonissue of 'How is This related to That?' When one focuses inward, one sees that This goeswith That in the same manner that flowers and bees gowith each other. We got so used to thinking of Metaphysics as 'Beyond' that we cannot think about it any other way, even when the truth stares us in the face. Doesn't it strike you as a bit odd that Metaphysical Truths are called 'Deeper Truths' while the area of Metaphysics is considered 'Outer'?

Our Common Confession

x>You have often referred to a Common Confession. What do you mean by that?

All Theologies, when delved into deeply enough, end up in the same unknown and it makes no sense to me to assume that one unknown is a separate Reality than any other unknown. One truth I have come to learn along this path is that no matter how you get there, there you are. The Totality of Truth includes that which is known and that which is unknown in which the more one comes to know, the more one realizes how much one does not know. There is truth about -O- in all Faiths, each of those truths is like the spokes of the wheel or the wall of the pot.

The Truth of -O- is like the hub of the wheel or the inside of the pot. If we are going to grant Infiniteness to -O-, the first thing one must do is confess there is no one totally accurate daffynition, for one cannot daffyfine the Infinite with a Finite. As Lao Tzu once commented, "Once you open your mouth, you are 186,000 miles off target." - to that I would like to add that being off to the left or right is still being off. No matter how many words we humans throw around, none of us, not even all of us combined, come anywhere close to a Precise Statement about -O-. Language can only take us so far, for words are nothing more than the paintings we hang on our mental walls in lieu of windows. If we wish to dip water, we need to cup our hands, not make fists.

All faiths have a school of thought within that can be called 'agnostic' in that it is freely confessed that ultimately, -O- is unknowable. They all freely confess that -O- Is Infinite. Where Theological difficulties arise is when we take a finite verbal formula and claim "This and Only This Formula is The Absolute Truth about Infinity." This is Idolatrous and dangerously close to Blasphemy as far as I'm concerned for by doing so, one limits the freedom of -O- to be what -O- will be. One spoke of the Wheel does not comprise the entire Wheel just as one instrument does not make up a Symphony Orchestra. -O- comes to us in the images we understand from our cultural upbringing in the same manner that St. Paul became all things to all men to draw them into the Church.

This Common Confession should be a cause for celebration between the World's Faiths as far as I'm concerned. In the long run, what matters is That we believe, not What we believe. I know -O- Is, beyond a shadow of a doubt, for I have yet to find anywhere -O- is not. I also know that any misunderstanding I may think I have of -O- is Incomplete and I take it as given that any -O-image is equally incomplete. This is not a cause for despair for my most joyful Confession is "-O- Is; the rest is Commentary." That -O- appears one way to you and another to me is an issue that Does Not Matter, what Does Matter is that He appears to both of us. Seeing as how both our misunderstandings of the Nature of -O- are equally incomplete, neither of us have the authority to play Spiritual oneupmanship.

x>x>This is not a cause for despair for my most joyful Confession is "-O- Is; the rest is Commentary." That -O- appears one way to you and another to me is an issue that Does Not Matter, what Does Matter is that He appears to both of us.
x>How is one to know the One True -O- if He appears to me, She appears to someone else, and as Nonbeingness to you?

The Reality beneath the differing images is the One True -O- and this Reality is ultimately unknowable in the sense that we cannot catch it in a net of words. I submit the drive to pin -O- down to one precise Theological daffynition is Idolatry and the drive to force others to accept that image is Blasphemous. There is quite a bit of difference between Classical and Reggae but at the core, both are forms of music just as Chinese and French are two forms of language. The differences between -O-images do not represent different -O-s as many people assume, but different misunderstandings of the One.
More than anything else, the main problem here is that people think of 'One' in the connotation of 'singular' whereas the 'Oneness' of -O- is 'manifold'. Saying that -O- is ultimately unknowable does not mean we cannot gnow quite a bit about that which by various names we all call -O-. We do not know everything about Physical Reality, but we can make estimates based on what we do know, which is the same thing we can do with Theological knowledge. The Infinite cannot be known by the Finite, it can only be pointed to by the Finite. We make a mistake when we mistake the finger pointing at the moon for the moon itself. Him is a Finite, Her is a Finite, and Nonbeingness is a Finite. The Source of 'Him', 'Her' and 'Nonbeingness' is Infinite.
The problem is compounded when we then link that assumption to the further assumption one can daffyfine the Infinite with the Finite. A theological common in all Religions is that whatever name is given, it is postulated -O- is Infinite and this is why I say the quest to daffyfine -O- is Idolatrous. How dare anyone think they can restrict the ability of -O- to be what -O- will be to their limited misunderstanding? If a person needs to envision -O- through the Christian image, that is what happens; if the image needs to be Buddhist, that is what

happens. Our friend over there sees Her and I see a somewhat Taoist image. What we could call the 'one true -O-' is the Source of all images, not any one image, in and of itself.

This is not to say the images are 'false', just that they are incomplete. Newtonian Mechanics is an incomplete view of physical reality, not 'false' in the sense it is 'wrong', merely that there are limits to the applicability of the theory. Seeing as how we are yakking about -O-, there are things about -O- that are beyond our Finite Knowledge, each -O-image is like a Newtonian point of view while the Source of all images is a Quantum point of view, or Gnowledge about the Infinite. I have said for a long time that Spirituality is food for the soul and I submit the passage above could be read as an analogy that no food, Physical or Spiritual is unclean. To say that Judaism is 'false' is the same as saying Chinese cuisine is 'false' as the former is in the spectrum of Spirituality while the latter is in the spectrum of Physical. Judaism is not the whole of Spirituality just as Chinese is not the whole of cuisine. A dive into hubris is the least one accomplishes when one assumes that one's particular confession is everyone's confession.

x>x>A theological common in all Religions is that whatever name is given, it is postulated -O- is Infinite and this is why I say the quest to daffyfine -O- is Idolatrous . . . What we could call the 'one true -O-' is the Source of all images, not any one image, in and of itself.

x>Are you implying they worship false idols?

Gosh no. A Christian -O-image is true for Christians, just as a Hindu -O-image is true for a Hindu; that which we call True is -O-. One -O-image is just as Incomplete as another -O-image for -O- is a Reality that cannot be defined, and this is due to the nature of Infinity. At one and the same time, -O- is the Jewish G-d, the Islamic Allah, the Christian God, the Hindu Brahman, the Buddhist Dharmakaya, the Tao, the feminine aspect in Wicca, and much more. Each carries within a bit of the truth, but The Truth cannot be found in one of them. I realize my -O-image is just as Incomplete as yours, how could I look down on yours and call it false? You see, the main problem we have with -O-images is that we have this concept of -O- as a Metaphysical or Theological issue, thinking of Metaphysics as 'outside' or 'beyond' Physics.

As far as I'm concerned, this is a backwards way of looking at it, for Physics is an 'outside' understanding of Reality while Metaphysics/Theology is an 'inside' understanding of Reality. A secondary problem is that we have a confusion in our definition of "Oneness" when it comes to -O-/Reality. We think of 'oneness' as 'singular' or 'exclusive' - this and only this is The Truth, rather than as 'manifold' or 'inclusive' - each is a representation of The Truth. The matter becomes further complicated by the assumption that Physical Reality and Metaphysical Reality are two separate Realities that have nothing to do with each other. The thing I have against a singular outlook is this restricts the Infinite to a Finite. This thinking limits the ability of -O- to be what -O- will be, for according to those who think of -O- as 'other', -O- cannot also be 'self', for that is a contradiction in terms.

My point is this; each Theological image is a Finite understanding of That which is Infinite. A Finite understanding is neither true nor false, it is Incomplete. Seeing as how there is no one 'true' -O-image; the idea of a 'false' -O-image does not make sense, for each is equally true and false. Each image is as Incomplete as every other image, which means each, is worthy of equal respect and we do -O- a grave disservice when we use our images as clubs to beat up on others. -O- appears to each of us in the manner that is best understood as a relationship between that person and -O-. I'm certainly not going to question why -O- approaches you in the Christian version and me in a somewhat Buddhist/Taoist version and I submit it is more conducive to peacefulness if we celebrate that -O- approaches each of us.

x>x>As far as I'm concerned, this is a backwards way of looking at it, for Physics is an 'outside' understanding of Reality while Metaphysics/Theology is an 'inside' understanding of Reality. A secondary problem is that we have a confusion in our definition of "Oneness" when it comes to -O-/Reality. We think of 'oneness' as 'singular' or 'exclusive' . . . rather than as 'manifold' or 'inclusive' . . . The matter becomes further complicated by the assumption that Physical Reality and Metaphysical Reality are two separate Realities that have nothing to do with each other.

x>These ideas seem to be central to your thinking.

They are results of what can only be talked about as a challenge from -O- when I was but a mere youth. Around the occurrence of the first of my mystical experiences I was attending Vacation Bible School in the local Baptist Church. The theme was The Crusades and we played roles in the Holy Army and built cardboard castles and all that. I could not get around the idea The All-Powerful needed an army to Do His Will and the image of the Old Man on The Throne with Eyes of Fire and a Sword for a Tongue taught in the Baptist Church and the Loving Shepherd image being taught by the Presbyterian Church I attended when I spent weekends at my grandparents.

At that stage, I hung in the camp that ascribed "One" as "Singular" and the two images I was getting looked like two different -O-s altogether. During my walks in the semi-developed land, I would ponder this kinda stuff; in a sense, asking -O- what He is. The answer came to me (Which I misunderstood at the time.) as 'I Am not That.', which has become clarified over the years to 'I Am not Just that.' From the very beginning there was never a doubt in my mind that -O- Is and the more I discover the Truth of 'not Just', the stronger the certainty becomes. Infinity is expressed through Manifoldness from the 'inside' and Singular from the 'outside' because the Nature of Infinity is Inclusive. In other words, 'one' and 'many' are different ways of talking about the same Reality, for it is all a matter of perspective. For example, because we look outward at the stars, we think we also look outward to -O-. One daffynition of Reality is that it is a sphere where Circumference and Center is no*where* and *now*here, or to paraphrase Jesus, there is no place we cannot find -O- when we seek.

That which we call -O- is the Source of the images and we all have That in common, no matter how we choose to yap about it. What you see as Lutheran is different than what x sees as a Wiccan, and yet still different than what our Hindu friend sees. Each of our -O-images are not images of 'different -O-s' as so many want to preach, each is a different perspective of the same Reality - That which is the Source of all images. The idea that -O- is a Reality 'outside' all this has always been a philosophical issue with me because He is 'not Just.' No matter how we talk about -O-, we all agree He is 'Root and Ground' of all phenomena, which means She is just as much 'inside' as He is 'outside' while That Which Is has no boundaries.

x>x>The answer came to me (Which I misunderstood at the time.) as 'I Am not That.', which has become clarified over the years to 'I Am not Just that.' . . . Infinity is expressed through Manifoldness from the 'inside' and Singular from the 'outside' because the Nature of Infinity is Inclusive . . . No matter how we talk about -O-, we all agree He is 'Root and Ground' of all phenomena, which means She is just as much 'inside' as He is 'outside' while That Which Is has no boundaries.

x>Why is it that although your basic -O-image is of Nonbeingness, you constantly use terms like "Him" and "Her" in your talks?

Not to be too sarcastic, but that's the Nature of The Beast. In order to understand anything, we must yap about it in terms we can comprehend. For example, atoms are not miniature solar systems, no matter how convenient it is to talk about them as if they were. The main reason I those terms like 'Him' and 'Her' are that this is the terminology most people use when discussing -O-, no matter what name they use. There are times when -O- can only be talked about in the Masculine and times when only the Feminine will do, just as there are times when neither suffice - it means that -O- is Aliveness/Beingness rather than being a Live Male or a Live Female Being. Look at it this way, we can talk about a male Human or a female Human, but Humanity is neither male nor female. Sometimes the only way to yap about some of these things is to talk about it as if -O- were a sentient being that does things, but when I talk that way, I'm thinking in terms of the 'nondoing' of Taoism.

So much of Reality is paradoxical it is somewhat safe to say that -O- has a fairly warped sense of humor. This humor has become quite evident to me during this mystical trip I've been on. Each Faith has a -O-image that is true, but the Truth cannot be found in any one of them, leading me to the conclusion that -O- is the Ultimate Paradox. If a person needs to 'find' -O- in the -O-image of the Jewish Faith, that is what that person receives and if a person needs a Hindu image, that is what they will get. One can almost say that -O- does it this way out of His Infinite Compassion, but to say 'He does it' is to invite the question of 'Why He does it.' This is a question that has only one answer, why not?

Life is a blend of emotional and intellectual aspects and we get lost in trivial details when we talk about 'why it is so.' Yapping about -O- as Nonbeing appeals to my mind but does little for my heart; on the other hand, yapping about -O- as Being appeals to my heart yet leaves my mind unsatisfied. By accepting the paradox at the center of a Radical Nondualist approach, both aspects are satisfied; I can talk about His Compassion and the mysterious Tao with equal Incompleteness for not one of them IS the Reality, which is -O-. There is no mistaking the image of Him slapping me upside the head when I mess up as being the Reality, it is a way of talking about it. One knows -O- with the mind and gnows -O- with the heart and the Truth is somewhere between.

Just as our misunderstanding about Physical Reality is based on Particle and Wave, our misunderstanding about Theological Reality is based on knowledge and gnowledge. No matter how intellectually satisfying the Nonbeing image, one needs the Complimentary image of Being for emotional satisfaction; to paraphrase Jesus, one loves -O- with all their heart and mind. With all images being equally Incomplete, I fully realize that any image I care to use simply cannot come close to conveying the Truth, no matter how much truth the statement contains.

The Centermost Reality

x>x>Does it really matter if there is no personal immortality or nonpersonal unmortality when one considers exactly what the Centermost Reality of one's Beingness actually is?

x>You keep talking about a 'Centermost Reality'. What are you talking about?

The Centermost Reality is the Unnamable That which is the center, from which Yin and Yang emanate. As we have discussed in the thread called "Panencarnation", the concept of the individual, eternally existent human soul is mistaken. Although I go by the name "Dino", that is not who I am underneath the mask that uses that name and in the same manner, who you are underneath your mask is not "x", but that selfsame Centermost Reality. One aspect of -O- is 'Otherness' but we make a category mistake when we image that 'Otherness' as an outside type of reality, for another aspect is called 'the root and ground' of existence, which is an inside type of reality. The Otherness of -O- is only so because -O- is not a Being, He is Beingness.

It is said in the Bible that the Heavens reflect the Glory of G-d and in a sense that is true, but they also emanate the Glory of -O-. In your Theology, this can be called the Holy Spirit, that which can barely be symbolized: No matter how we choose to image -O-, at the center of the image, we all find the same reality. The Tao, the Dharma, G-d, Allah, Brahman, God, these and the many more are all but names we place over the Reality so we can talk about it in our stumbling fashion. -O- the Holy Spirit is indwelling and there is nowhere it is not. There is, ultimately, no reality but -O- and everything else is window dressing for the show.

x>What does it mean that Humanity is a pattern of energy evolving into Consciousness? What does it mean that A human is a mask -O- wears in the Cosmic Drama? This all seems to deny the validity and worth of the individual, making this all meaningless.

The problem with the Western approach is that it looks for meaning from the outside as if the parts explain the whole rather than looking at it as the whole is pointed to by the parts. We look at the individual as an end result rather than a continuing process. Rather than denying the validity and worth of the individual, it is another story about Who/What the individual is. Our uniqueness arises from our commonness in that the individual is a spotlight in what could be daffyscribed as the 'Infinite Mind of -O-.' I know there are some who are going to take this wrong, but one way to look at it is like ex-mayor Ed Koch walking around asking the people how he was doing. Sometimes I can only daffyscribe Reality as -O- walking around asking the same thing while playing the ultimate game of Hider/Seeker.

A mistake is made when we look for the meaning of all this from the outside in for when looks at it from an inside out perspective, the individual is elevated to Divine Status. Looking from the inside, Humanity is the Universe come Alive and Aware (from the perspective of earth) from one point of view, and from another, each of us is a Living Icon of -O-. What does it mean that each of us is a living icon of -O-? For one, it means that no one person is intrinsically better than another. The Divine Spark is the Central Reality of each and every one of us, even though we have differing images of the Divine. We are no better than the worst of us and no worse than the best of us. To paraphrase an old Taoist story - Heaven went through all it did to provide you with a body and you use it to argue about "hard" and "white."

When one talks about a Human as a mask -O- wears, one is not denying the value of the individual, one is looking at the individual from another perspective. As far as I'm concerned, I find the image of Humans as fallen creatures to be degrading when in actuality, each of us is an Icon of -O-. Underneath this thingie I call "Dino" and underneath the thingie you call "X" is the self-same Reality that is nowhere and nowhere. I am not afraid of death for I know that i was dead before i was born while I do not experience birth and death. In a sense, the Western idea that each of us has but one life to live is true, but this is a limited truth in that after "i" die, "I" will reincarnate, but "i" will stay in the mind of -O-. Whatever this energy that calls itself Dino is will be recycled just as all other forms of energy in the universe will be recycled. The chance that the resulting pattern of the recycling process would produce a direct copy of the pattern that is "me" in "my" next lifecycle is astronomically small but it is not impossible.

x>x>Underneath this thingie I call "Dino" and underneath the thingie you call "X" is the self-same Reality that is nowhere and nowhere. I am not afraid of death for I know that i was dead before i was born while I do not experience birth and death.

x>How can you not be afraid of dying?

I didn't say anything about dying, I talked about being dead. Like anyone, I hope my death come easily; the point is that I know that someday it will take place. If I had my druthers, I would just as soon die in my sleep, but I got a hunch -O- is going to have one of His Practical Jokes in store for me. There was a time before my birth, which as far as I'm concerned, is the same type of state of existence as that state of existence called death.

Once upon a time i was 'dead' and then i was 'alive', a time will come when i will be 'dead' again, but the I within 'me' does not undergo this. It is this 'within' that is the Centermost Reality that cannot die because it is never born and is more 'me' than this wacko I call "Dino" can ever be. This is not to deny 'my' importance in the overall scheme of things any more than a character an actor has played is unimportant - i am a Living Icon of -O-, with all the tremendous responsibilities that come with it. Beyond that, it is the recognition the Centermost Reality of 'you' is the same, for Unity is both Singular and Manifold.

At a time when I was getting heavy into studying various mystical paths, I ran across a saying in the Don Juan books about using death as your advisor. The statement surprised me for a bit, then I thought about it and realized the value of what was being said; it becomes real hard to act stupid while one is acting as if each moment is the last one they have. One of the things I have come to realize over the years, both through personal experience and in discussion with others, is that one feels the most alive when they are in immediate danger - when death is walking by one's side. It is at those times when one's vision is the clearest, one's mind is working on all eight cylinders at full speed, and one is intensely focused on RIGHT NOW!!!

By treating each moment as if it is the last one you will have, each act is potentially your last and I'm not sure about you but I would rather be remembered fondly. I find that if I can treat my death as my advisor, I'm less likely to shoot from the lip only to hit myself in the foot. Don't let all my blather lead you to assume that I have adequate control over my immediate responses; I have a tendency to be rather to the point when I let the dragon run loose. I realize we have discussed this before, but this attitude about death as advisor does not bring about despair because in living this way, each moment is precious in and of itself.

x>x>In the West we have this hope of an endless existence in Heaven after physical death and in the East we have a hope of an endless nonexistence in Nirvana after physical death . . . I suggest both approaches miss the point. The goals of Eternal Immortality in Heaven and Eternal Unmortality in Nirvana are equal mistakes.

x>This time I think I'm lost.

If the Earth is an example of how the rest of the Universe does its business, there must be a huge amount of life out there. No matter where we look on this planet, there are living organisms, and to conclude life arose on this one planet alone

---

is absurd. From the sheer number of living organisms on this planet, one could come to the conclusion that one of the functions of the planet is to produce life. When I use the term 'functions', I'm not talking about a mechanical process as if it were some factory spitting out widgets. This is something the Earth does of itself, like a flower growing from a seed.

One thing we must keep in mind that it does not matter if we are discussing the smallest semi living virus or the largest organism, each have one thing in common, if one can call life a 'thing', but you get my point. A dead whale and a dead virus have the same physical components as the other half of the story but there is a vital something missing that is common to both. Life can be manifested as a bacterium just as it can as a human and we are constantly finding new examples of life in extreme environments. It is absurd to think this something we call life in a human is somehow other than this something we call life in a rabbit. Yes there are differences between being a rabbit and being a human but the point is they are both living beings, sharing that something vital with each other and the aforementioned whale and virus. What is this something we all have in common?

The physical aspect of our existence is one commonality. Both a human and a virus are composed of physical matter and that physical matter is composed of patterns of something we cannot daffyfine yet. The mental aspect of our existence is one commonality as well. The soul is a pattern of something we cannot daffyfine yet either. I submit that if two somethings are equally unknown, it is safe to assume they are but aspects of the same something. That something in one human is the same something that is in another human. If our 'soul' is a totally unique and eternally existing reality, there are some awkward questions to ask.

One is 'where were we prior to our existence?' For years I have tried to think of something along the lines of a huge storage locker where our souls are stored until it is our time to play in the sun. This would require another storage locker for those who have come in out of the rain and I cannot see that being the case, given that recycling seems to be the universal order of the day. We are right in saying each human is unique, but we are wrong in assuming said uniqueness is an eternal condition. That hidden self I mentioned above is the same something I labeled the centermost reality earlier in this discussion. It seems that -O- enjoys physical existence and the mystical experience is rightly called 'Ecstatic', although I would prefer a term like 'Ecdynamic' for the experience is far from static. Despite the fact the experience contains common features, it never is the same twice in a row, each building on others.

I have no idea why -O- chose physical existence in a human body (at least here on Earth), but I will not despair over His choice for to do so is sacrilegious. Your complaint reminds me of a painting I read about once about three reactions to tasting vinegar - one complained that it tasted sour, one complained that it tasted bitter, and one said it tasted like vinegar, just like it is supposed to. As it is said somewhere in Taoist texts - Heaven went through all this trouble to give you a body and you yap about 'hard and white.' This is why I disagree with the goals of eternal Heavenly existence and eternal Nirvanic nonexistence; one approach runs away because vinegar is not honey and the other approach runs away because of the bad taste vinegar leaves in one's mouth. Both approaches completely miss the point that vinegar is supposed to taste like vinegar, not like wine or a candy bar.

Yes, there is pain and suffering entailed with physical existence and yes, life is temporary. Be that as it may, have you really considered what it would be like to be alive forever (supposing for the sake of the argument that we have eliminated all forms of pain and suffering)? I don't care how beautiful they are, sunsets must get boring after the first thousand billion. We both like a nice steak dinner, but I wonder how long we could stand it as a steady diet. Eventually one would learn everything there is to learn and then one would run out of surprises.

One of my downfalls in College was that I kept finding interesting classes that were not directly related to the degree and taking them for the sheer joy of learning something new. My ex-wife used to complain that I was moving on because I got bored, but it wasn't like that - I just kept on finding pretty pebbles in the sand. Many of my professors used to tell me that if I weren't careful, I would end up becoming a professional student. The Ceramics instructors lamented jokingly that I only came there to get my head out of the clouds and my hands in the mud. This spilled over into my life after I left college, where I have pretty much drifted from job to job through Temp Agencies. Everywhere I went, I found interesting aspects to the job, pretty pebbles by the banks of the river as it were, and that enthusiasm for learning new things has led me to become a 'professional temp'.

The point of the above little aside is that if one wishes to consider each new field of study or job a new life, it is somewhat analogous to the Cycle of Life and Death. -O- keeps coming back to learn and experience new things in a never-ending cycle where He does it in all places at the same time. Just as nutrients are recycled in the physical to fertilize new growth, mentrients are recycled in the spiritual/mental to fertilize new growth. A Tree may only live for a certain amount of time but the Orchard continues just as a Human lives for a certain amount of time but Humanity continues. We are, in a manner of speaking, going against the will of -O- by the running away to an Eternity Somewhere Else.

We need not despair for all this is -O- and whatever happens will happen. Rather than mope about temporality, consider that eternity only lasts the lifetime of a single individual while the Eternal continues. There is no point in complaining

---

about change when change is what spurs growth and keeps everything new. It does not matter that you personally will not receive your Reward for doing good in the afterlife because afterlife and beforelife are merely relative to the Eternal Now. One makes a mistake in assuming that meaning must come from an outside agency in the same manner that 'law' implies 'lawgiver'. The fact of randomness as a central 'working' of the quantum level of reality does not mean that life has no purpose, for like 'meaning'; 'purpose' comes from within. Likewise, we need not run from a natural course of events just because we do not like certain aspects of it. It seems like the business of Reality is to make more points of view of itself. As the saying is misquoted - 'The eyes are the windows of Reality.' and as we all know, a person can look in a window as well as out. It seems to me that we commit sacrilege with our attitude about existence; we condemn and run away from that which we should be celebrating. -O- becomes aware through each human being . . . One way to describe it is that -O- sees through our eyes, hears through our ears, speaks through our mouths, and so forth, to continue the above quote beyond talking about Earth. This does not mean that I'm advocating traditional hedonism - "Eat, drink, and be merry, for tomorrow we die." Doing so would be going to the other extreme, which is just as much a mistake. As I've been saying all along, life is a balance and it is only rare cases where one extreme or the other is in control. We need to treat the physical aspect of life with the respect it deserves, no more and no less. Sister Mind needs Brother Ass just as much as Brother Ass needs Sister Mind for we cannot have one without the other. Neither gluttony nor asceticism carried to extreme can be done to the glory of -O-. As Jesus pointed out, one must eat in order to be able to observe the Law, but, if one is stuffed to the point of lethargy, one cannot observe the Law either.

x>x> Somehow we fail to realize that it is through the physical that the spiritual becomes evident.
x>I'm not sure what you are trying to say here.

My complaint about most traditions is what I see as a lack of perspective when it comes to Brother Ass. For whatever reason, it has turned out that here on Earth, Mind/Body goeswith in a seamless unity that extends from the 'smallest' subatomic particle to the Universe as a whole. It does us no good to complain about the changeability and temporary nature of physicality, as it would not change the facts of existence, as we know it. We miss the point when we degrade Brother Ass because sometimes he lets us down; just because some men do evil things that do not mean that all men will do evil things. The opposite is true as well in that although some people are saintly, not all are, so Sister Mind sometimes lets us down. By concentrating on the extremes, we ignore the means and the overwhelming majority of people are decent folks, despite the rascality in each of us.

In our confusion over Mind/Body or Spiritual/Material, we have a tendency to lean towards the 'side' of Mind and Spiritual and tolerate the other 'side' as little as possible. The sides only exist linguistically - 'brain' and 'mind' are two ways of talking about the same reality. As I have talked about elsewhere, in a dualism, we cannot have one without other. Take one 'side' away and the other 'side' will vanish as well - modify one, the other modifies in response; consider what it would be like if all the bees in the world were to suddenly vanish. We need to recognize that if we existed in a different form, our concept of spiritual would be different as well for physical/spiritual is the same goeswith in the same seamless unity. We further compound the error when we conceive of the individual human soul or ego as central to our existence and this is because we are confused over the concept of individual. As far as I have been able to tell, there is only one reality that fits the daffynition of 'individual' and that is the totality we choose by various names to call -O- and that is the Centermost Reality of all. It makes absolutely no sense to degrade Brother Ass because it does exactly what it is supposed to. We might as well treat the vessel -O- has come up with to become aware through the perspective of Earth with the respect it deserves. In a manner of speaking, it is just as blasphemous to disrespect physicality as it is to disrespect spirituality, as both are of the selfsame unity. I have this odd feeling that if I could ask -O- Why concerning physicality, His answer would be Why Not?

This is why I contend the two traditional approaches are mistaken, for the universe "peoples", trees "apple", and although a person or a tree dies, Humanity, Orchards, and Life go on in a constant state of change. Hoping for eternal existence in Heaven denies Life from one extreme while hoping for eternal nonexistence in Nirvana denies it from another. It is the eternal part of both equations that is one aspect of the mistake, for nothing except -O- is eternal. All Reality, Physical and Mental, is compounded and as the Buddha said, "All compounded things are subject to dissolution." Another aspect of the mistake is the assumption that Heaven and Nirvana are realities somewhere else, while the truth of the matter is that Heaven is a glance over the right shoulder while Nirvana is a glance over the left. It is true that each of us has but one life to live, but that is because -O- is an actor that cannot be typecast. It is also true the suffering we entail is the result of what happen in earlier lifecycles, but the answer does not lie in breaking one's ties to the Wheel of Life.

There is no reason to assume that we can get off the Wheel just because we do not enjoy the cost of the ticket. We can work together to make the situation here on Earth less painful. We can join together to eliminate terrorism. If we put our minds to it, we can eliminate hunger throughout the world. Monetary motives need not be the primary drive for the Pharmaceutical Industry's distribution of medicines. We can work to ease conflict no matter where it may arise. We can work to achieve true equality between all humans in all phases of life. Yes there are situations that make me sad. But to let those things overshadow the joy that can also be found in life is to miss the point entirely. All along I have been talking about balance and this applies here as well. Sometimes life is wonderful and sometimes it is a pain in the ass, sorta like a wobbling top that refuses to fall over.

I'm not suggesting we go to the other extreme and make an Idol out of Physicality, for Human Life is a balance between the Spiritual and Physical Realms. Just as Awareness is the Spiritual aspect of -O-, Body is the Physical aspect and is therefore just as Holy, deserving the same respect. We do great disrespect to -O- when we denigrate the vessel He has chosen because it does not measure up to our standards. Physicality is not evil, not a burden to bear, not a result of blind, random interaction, not a hindrance to Enlightenment and death is the natural result of Life, not the result of a supposed 'Original Sin' committed by my supposed ancestor.

Celebrating our physicality does not mean we can throw off all moral guidelines and behave in any manner we wish; one can enjoy food without being a glutton and wine without becoming a drunk, in other words. If one remains exclusively in the Spiritual, one misses out on the beauty to be found in the Physical and exclusively remaining in the Physical becomes a cheap thrill after a while.

x>x>One can almost say that -O- does it this way out of His Infinite Compassion, but to say 'He does it' is to invite the question of 'Why He does it.' This is a question that has only one answer, why not? . . . we get lost in trivial details when we talk about 'why it is so.'
x>I fail to see how the reasons -O- does things are "trivial".

When we start talking along the lines of -O- 'having a reason' for doing something, we think of -O- as a reasoning Being. For example, He created Humans to worship Him. This is our reasoning about why He did it and may or may not be accurate. For all we know, we may just be interesting pets that keep Him amused. Alan Watts gives a little ditty about Heaven as question and answer period wherein everybody gets a chance to ask -O- a question, which I paraphrase.

One person asks "Why is the Sky blue?" and -O- goes into a detailed lecture concerning the visual range of electromagnetic energy and the effect Earth's atmosphere has on it. After a few seconds silence, someone in back asks -O- "Why blue?" to which He replies "Because."

Does it Really Matter that -O- appears to me one way, you another, and our buddy over there another? I see no reason why we should quibble over the details of how -O- appears to each of us; it is what it is and there is nothing we can do to change it. This is where thinking of -O- as a Being falls short of the Glory that is -O-.

x>x>This is where thinking of -O- as a Being falls short of the Glory that is -O-.
x>How does it fall short?

When we image -O- as a being, we limit His ability to be what She Will Be. An image is a finite construct; -O- is neither Finite nor construct. The Glory of -O- is not that He appears to you as G-d, but that She appears to our friend over there as Goddess, to me as Tao, and to our friend over yonder as Allah, all at the same time. The Infinity that is -O- cannot be limited to one image for an image is but a pointer towards the Reality. My -O-image is no more and no less a pointer than yours is, and yours is no more or less that our friends' over there. There are Eternal truths and there are Relative truths - that "-O- *is*" belongs in the former while -O- as Allah is in the latter. There is nothing Divine about a Being that one can fully Know and I gotta say that IF -O- were that simplistic, I would be disappointed.

x>But notice how you define the Atman; it's a gulf of difference between that and the concept of the individual soul in Judaism, Christianity, and Islam. And since this was originally a post on the question of whether religions could unify, I find that gulf to be unbridgeable except by theological conquest.

What's wrong with peaceful coexistence? As fellow travelers on the path to -O-, what need is there for conquest? I see no reason why we can't all agree to disagree on certain matters and celebrate the things we have in common. The concept that there is One True Faith™ that has to conquer all others is repelling. It seems to me that if we all sing the same song in Heaven, it would get boring in a few millennia. There is diversity throughout the natural world and it is my contention there is diversity in Heaven as well - is not the material world an icon of the spiritual world in the same manner that, as Orthodox Christians believe, humans are icons of -O-? This is an area where the thesaurus approach to Religion would be of great value. All too many of us depend solely on a dictionary approach, not realizing that although the concept of Salvation is understood differently by a Jew, a Christian, a Buddhist, and a Hindu, the thesaurus meaning of the term is the same.

In my humble opinion, attempting to take everything in the Bible as literal is as wrong as discounting it solely for the literal mistakes in it. Of course, this applies equally to the texts of all Traditions. The way I look at it is that literalists have butterfly collections while figurativists have collections of photographs of butterflies. I prefer live butterflies, myself. One way of looking at it is that Literalists have dead facts and the Figurativists have pretty images. In clinging to what they hold sacred, they miss the reality of What Is.

x>Hmm, I 'spose so. It's just in whatever context you take it. I think I'm wasting my time trying to convert Jews to Christianity. Maybe when I have as much bible knowledge as them, I will be able to. I would just like to say that I know Jesus died for me cos the Holy Spirit is in me and that's that!

Why convert them? Judaism is a valid Religion, Christianity is a valid Religion, Buddhism is a valid Religion, etc. If the song of -O- were to be reduced to one voice, much beauty would be lost.
A little example from classical music, I am fond of Bach's Toccata and Fugue in Dminor. It is quite awesome to hear from a big pipe organ. Once I heard the piece after it had been transposed to an entire symphonic piece. The difference was like going from beauty to BEAUTY. Monotones are not music. This is a typical Western Christian attitude, becoming more militant the further one gets into Protestantism - everyone must convert, which is an attitude no other Faith takes. Can you imagine how flat Gregorian chant would sound if all the voices were identical? The beauty of the Chant is in the harmonious blend of different voices. Heck, we all have, at one time or another, had to put up with someone who spoke at great length in a monotone - remember how quickly we got tired of listening to it?

x>I would hope that you are following the path you have chosen to follow because you believe it to be right - even though it may not be. If a person is not following what he thinks is the truth, what is the point in following it? And, if you don't think the path you're following really is the truth, what's the point?

I believe my path is true for me - I have been following what I feel is what -O- laid out for me and me alone. I am willing to admit that I may be mistaken about what I feel -O- has written on my heart, but I am also not going to go against the internalized teaching. For me to think my path is the One True Path to -O- for everyone is something I cannot do and maintain my spiritual integrity. To go from San Diego to L.A., The Way To Get There depends on How One Wishes To Travel. One can go by car, take a plane, go by boat . . . Western Faiths can be viewed as going by bus while the Eastern Faiths prefer to walk. Some of us prefer to blaze our own trails through the countryside, rejoicing when we cross paths with others.

x>It would seem to me that according to your definition, these words of Christ are either wrong or mistaken, or bashing of other people's beliefs?

No, we merely have different understandings. It is not what Jesus taught that is the cause of bashing, IMHO. I submit it is the Christology of Pauline Christianity that leads to this behavior. While I wholeheartedly agree with the Sermon on the Mount, I cannot accept that He is the only Messenger.

I am not saying that I feel the philosophy of Jesus as being -O- incarnate is false/wrong. My claim is that to say it only happened in Him and the fate of my soul depends on accepting the proper Christological daffynition is Hubris and, to me, is an incomplete understanding of -O-. Neither am I saying that my understanding is more complete than yours. You and I both believe that, ultimately -O- is One and is Creator - that we have different daffynitions is, to me, secondary. We can agree to disagree on what we have in difference and celebrate what we have in common.

We all agree that, in the final analysis, -O- is One. Although we are in agreement on this, we all have a differing daffynition of this Oneness. Are these different daffynitions of different realities or are they just different daffynitions of the same reality?

The Science versus Religion Nonissue

x>x>Traditional monism completely misses the obvious.
x>What do you mean?

The traditional monistic method of solving the problem of dualism is to pick one side of the issue as real and the other as unreal. No matter how finely crafted our arguments for our sides are we always are left with what I call a 'yes, but . . . ' feeling; for example, the Mind/Body nonissue. The assumption is made that because 'mind' and 'body' are different types of whatevers, they are different Types of whatevers. It is this concept of 'separateness' that is one cause of the problem for the separation is logical, not existential.

A flower is different than a bee, but without one, the other would be quite different, in order for an electrical circuit to be functional, there must be a positive and a negative working together and in order to be valid currency, a coin must not be two-headed. Mind is different than Body but they are manifestations of the same Reality just as electromagnetism requires both electric and magnetic fields. There is no barrier between 'mind' and 'body', there is what can be crudely talked about as an innerreaction of that which is called 'physical' and that which is called 'mental', neither being Ultimately Real™, in and of themselves. Neither 'side' gives rise to the 'other' as they are mutually dependent on each other for definition, for one cannot have the concept of 'long' with the concept of 'short' for contradistinction.

Related to this confusion is the concept of 'oneness', which we take for granted as a singular, exclusive state. Granted there is a modicum of truth in this but it is a partial truth for 'oneness' is a manifold, inclusive state as well. It all depends on how you look at it; from the heads or the tails 'side', it is still the same coin. This is because we have a tendency to think of metaphysical realities as 'outside' or 'beyond' physical Reality. The 'One' of traditional thinking is 'outside' and other than being creator has no relationship to all this, an Exclusive Oneness. An Inclusive Oneness is 'inside' and is intimately involved as the source of all this. By definition 'one' must be inclusive or else we end up with 'two' which combine to make 'three' and from there we get to numbers that boggles the imagination. The source is Inclusive while the image is Exclusive, the former existential and the latter logical.

All these are indications of the failure of Traditional Monism to recognize it is doing nothing more than choosing the pretty pebble in the left hand and tossing the pretty pebble in the right out with the rest of the pretty pebbles. Truth cannot be found in a singular pretty pebble of the mind for each pretty pebble contains a bit of the truth. As far as I'm concerned, Monism is nothing more than lopsided Dualism. The Truth of the Mind/Body discussion is not 'mind only' nor is it 'body only', it is somewhere between, much like a 'wavicle' is between a particle and a wave.

x>x>I submit the 'War between Science and Religion' is a false dichotomy—Science and Religion have nothing to fear from each other as they are complimentary rather than combative. Discoveries in Science raise questions about Biblical Theology, causing a tiff between the camps: the Biblical Literalist searches the Book and thinks he has found Life while the proponent of Scienceism (Science Literalist) confuses lack of evidence for the Biblical God to be lack of evidence for any -O-image.

x>At least you're an equal opportunity critic in this area.

Does the Uncertainty Principle question the existence of -O- or does it question a premise about -O- based on the Bible? Why does it mean that if the Biblical Daffynition is wrong in some respects that all -O-images are wrong? If, as we agree, -O- is Infinite, how can a finite formula (i.e. the Biblical) be adequate to the task? The quibble between these two camps is over things that are said about, not the existence of the Reality. In other words, this is a logical, not an existential, quandary.

Contrary to what the vocal few who promote this issue want us to believe, one can have both Spiritual and Scientific world images without being contradictory. The knowledge of why the sky is blue only prompts one to ask -O- 'why blue?' Lack of physical evidence for the existence of -O- results from looking outside for the cause rather than inside for the source. That which we call 'outside' could not exist without that which we call 'inside' while 'cause' and 'source' is a chicken-and-egg type of question. Spirituality is the hub while Science consists of the spokes and Religion functions as the rim on the Wheel of Reality. I have never understood why it is assumed that one must have either a Religious or a Scientific outlook on Reality, especially Western Religious and Western Scientific.

The Biblical and Science Literalists are equally hubristic by acting as if they have the authority speak for all of us on these matters. I find it somewhat amusing to listen to the arguments between the two camps as these people make idols out of images in their attempt to force all people to accept one or the other of the campfire stories as Truth. The Bibleist says only X is true while the Scienceism apologist says only Y is true and both fail to realize their respective images are irrelevant when it comes to Reality, which is at least A through Z. There is no reason to assume the Biblical Creation Story is more than headlines for the story of evolution, which started with the Big Bang, by the way. I agree with the concept of evolution but I do not agree with it being a blind, stupid process taking place in a blind and stupid Universe. I agree with the concept of creation, but I see it is an ongoing thingie rather than something that happened back in the past.

At one extreme, a rainbow is red and at the other blue, with neither red nor blue being total descriptions of the rainbow. A rainbow comprises a wide spectrum of colors that as a whole we call 'white.' The Whole is the Ultimate Reality while the 'parts' are Relative Reality. A net is useful for catching fish, but a net is a blend of openings and closings. One would not be able to use a room that consisted of solid walls and the wiring for the house requires both supply and return.

x>x>The quibble between these two camps is over things that are said about, not the existence of the Reality. In other words, this is a logical, not an existential, quandary . . .
x>This is an interesting point of view.

Let us take the story of God's Omniscience - on one side we have the campfire story that God Knows All while on the other side we have the campfire story that the Uncertainty Principle rules out Omniscience, and therefore the existence of God. On the Religion side of this particular spitting contest, all -O-images other than Christian are labeled 'false', despite there being many disagreements as to the 'acceptable' image throughout Christianity. It is Hubristic in the extreme to assume the -O-image of Christian Biblical Literalism be the -O-image that all peoples Must Have. On the same token, evolutionary theory need not mean that all peoples must follow Scietheism, an assumption just as hubristic. It seems to me this is a false dichotomy with equally unreasonable choices.

It does not follow that if some parts of one -O-image are shown to be mistaken from a Scientific P.O.V., that all -O-images are thereby invalid for the same reasons. The -O-image of Taoism does not include Omniscience so the idea of Quantum Uncertainty poses no threat. While Eastern campfire stories talk about -O- being all knowing, it more like how we know how we grow our hair or digest our food. Religion cannot 'prove' or 'disprove' scientific theory in the same manner that Science cannot 'prove' nor 'disprove' theological theory.

—

Although they are two aspects of the same enterprise (the understanding of Reality), they occupy different functions in life. Religion is in the sphere of the Intuitive while Science is in the sphere of the Rational.

In one respect, -O- is Omniscient but in another respect, there is no He Who Knows. If one were to assume -O- has a mind that we can somewhat comprehend, it would be something along the line of thought that He Knows in the same way we know how to digest our food. All Uncertainty brings into question is the -O-image of the Self Aware Being and all evolutionary theory brings into question is a Literal interpretation of the Bible. This does not mean, as has been bandied about over the length of this argument, that -O- is a delusion. Hinduism has long held the idea that -O- is not A Self Aware Being and the Universe to be evolutionary and changing.

This is why traditional monism misses the point, the One is not a choice between two sides of an issue. Unity is a Reality that encompasses Is and Is Not, sorta like saying there are three ways of looking at it. We act as if our dictionary daffynitions are the only valid ones, which is certainly not the case, for neither the Biblical nor the Scietheistic images cover the entirety of the Reality. One does not have to give up the idea of -O- just because Scientific evidence shows the universe to be self-generating. A true Monistic Theism is not One of Many, but One within Many, just as light is a rainbow of colors.

x>x>It seems to me this is a false dichotomy with equally unreasonable choices.

x>I have to tell you that I have never heard this issue talked about from this direction.

It seems a bit absurd to me that our Worldview be based on either one or the other when neither option fills the bill by itself. One might as well expect to win the marathon while running using only one leg or on being an expert skeet shooter with a lack of depth perception. As I've said all along, I submit this issue is nothing more than a long running spitting contest between a few radicals who cannot see that while one side is talking about the head of the coin, the other is talking about the tail of the very same coin.

The issue is not about Science versus Religion, it is about biblical based theology on one hand. The stars changing their positions in the sky says nothing about the existence of -O- as the most it says is that He did not assign permanent, fixed positions to the stars. All evolutionary theory questions is the biblical based assumption that God created everything in its' modern form. The only thing geology brings into doubt is the biblical based assumption the Earth is a mere six thousand years old. On the other hand, it is about an erroneous assumption that if there are doubts about the Biblical image of God that all -O-images are wrong as well, guilt by association in other words. There is no reason to assume that because Science 'proves' God is not Omniscient, that the concept of -O- is wrong. The stars have their orbits without being ordered around by the Tao and Brahma does not tell water to flow downhill.

I highly doubt if the spokespeople on either side of this stop to consider the lack of grandeur of the image of Reality they are attempting to foist upon us. The Christian God is the Ultimate Neighborhood Bully; either believe in Him or spend eternity in Hell. The Universe and all in it is nothing more than a flawed creation tainted by evil. The Universe is nothing but a collection of Stupid, Dead Matter reacting blindly to Physical Law. Out of all Eternity, Reality will have a beginning and an end; Religiously at Creation and whenever He rolls up the sidewalks, Scientifically at the Big Bang and we have yet to decide about the end. If we are flawed creations, the Fault is His for creating us this way. If the Universe is blind and stupid, I fail to understand how it could possibly come up with a critter that could make that statement.

I see no compelling reason why I should accept either answer. I cannot accept the Biblical based image of God but that does mean I reject the -O- concept. I agree the Universe is random at the quantum level but I fail to see how that makes the Universe blind and stupid. Our behavior is not 'caused' by heredity nor environment alone although each does limit our choices somewhat; we are neither predetermined nor are we completely free. To live exclusively in the Mind is just as imbalanced an approach to life as is living exclusively in the Physical and doing so makes one less human as far as I'm concerned.

x>x>The quibble between these two camps is over things that are said about, not the existence of the Reality. . . . This is why traditional monism misses the point, the One is not a choice between two sides of an issue.

x>You have also said that traditional dualism misses the point. Why do you think these approaches miss the point?

Traditional dualism misses by assuming the extremes are separate realities while traditional monism misses by picking one extreme over the other. The dualism is apparent - particles and waves are not 'two somethings', they are 'one something else' doing two dances at the same time.

I submit this is all tied to how we view metaphysical issues. What people fail to take into account is that metaphysics is an inside joke. People have a habit of assuming 'heaven' is an 'outside' reality. Whatever the agency in charge of all this is, it is The Source which all things come from as well as The Destination where all things go to in a cyclic dance of Bliss and there is no reason to assume Source and Destination are different places or realities. There is an aspect of Metaphysics that is outside and an aspect that is inside, neither being the truth, the whole truth, and nothing but the truth. We consider a metaphysical truth a 'deeper' truth, so why do we assume Metaphysical Truth is 'outside' Reality? One somewhat clumsy way of describing this is that this is a logical paradox rather than an existential state of being.

On one hand, light behaves as if it were made of particles, that being the only logical explanation and on the other hand, it behaves like waves, with that being the only logical explanation. The paradox is that light itself is neither what we call particle nor what we call wave, it is another can of worms called wavicle. From one direction, the validity of the 'mind only' argument is obvious and from the other, the 'matter only' argument works; it all depends on how one chooses to look at the issue. Neither side is Truth as 'mind' and 'matter' are different patterns of the same we know not what. This we know not what is the Reality, not "Particle" or "Wave", the latter two being descriptions of what Reality is doing. "Mind" is the explanation for the nonphysical, and "Body" is the explanation for the physical aspect of life. Life itself is a balance of what we call 'mind' and what we call 'body' just as 'mind' is a balance between Rationality and Intuitiveness. In an expansion of 'the name is not the thing' concept, one must also conclude 'the explanation is not the thing' as well. The "One" and the "Many" are the same Reality explained from different directions.

x>x>What people fail to take into account is that metaphysics is an inside joke.
x>I'm not sure what you mean here.

The joke is that there is ultimately no difference between one side of a dichotomy and the other. Without 'long', we would not have 'short' in contradistinction. Is 'left' the enemy of 'right' or is it the case they support each other? While our attention is caught up in the drama of choosing between door A and door B, we fail to notice door C. The first door gives us a left handed, the second a right handed, the third gives us an ambidextrous, image of Reality. The monism of door A or B is a choice of one image of a logical dualism over another and as Lao Tzu quipped 'choosing is a sickness of the mind.' We say Reality itself is one or the other, but is that really the case?

Saying so is not always the case as light and platypi show us. Light may look white, but it is red, blue, green, and violet at the same time. A mammal nurses its young and a reptile lays eggs - the platypus does both, so we had to come up with a new daffynition. It was once said the Universe could be completely explained in Newtonian terms; now we know that sometimes one must use quantum terms. Some claim heredity is the prime mover, some claim environment, both ignore the whole story of a balance between Nature and Nurture. It used to be said that if a human traveled at sixty miles an hour, they would be crushed. At onetime it was thought the world was flat and was the center of the universe.

Atoms were once imaged as miniature solar systems, now the most accurate is clouds of probability.

One can adequately explain Reality as 'mind' just as well as 'body' as long as one ignores the 'yes, but . . .' questions implicit in each stance. The problem in ignoring what this constant questioning means is that we never get around questioning the idea that the answer must be one or the other. Neither stance is The Truth no matter how much truth it entails. Rather than the dichotomy of coexisting 'mind' and 'body', what is happening is a 'mind/body' symbiotic relationship, for without 'body' as we understand it, we would not have 'mind' as we understand it. If we were not equipped to see the wavelength of light called 'red', we would have no concept of the color red. If Reality is 'matter', how come we can make sense of it? Likewise, if it is 'mind', what is causing the impressions?

Menus and Meals

x>x> -O- is and the rest is commentary . . . -O- is the Ultimate Paradox . . . All -O-images are Incomplete . . . Thinking there is One True Confession confuses belief in a particular -O-image with faith in the Isness of the Source of the -O-images . . . Not only is -O- grander than we imagine, -O- is grander than we can imagine . . .

x>I have been reading your conversations for some time now. I have to confess I have a different take on what you are saying now as opposed to then. At first I assumed your 'Incompleteness' concept was a slam against religion in general. What I see now is a critique of a religious attitude in particular. You criticize the idea that a group has a truth for everyone, yet you are doing the same, are you not?

As paradoxical as it sounds, I am, with the difference being that I'm yapping that -O- is while others yap about what -O- is. I propose these ideas for consideration and further discussion, for as I've often said, Spirituality is a uniter in that we believe, while Theology is a divider in what we believe. There has been talk in some Christian circles of an 'ecumenical movement' as if this concept is purely Christian. These people are looking at the idea in a limited scope by doing it this way. If we take ecumenical to its logical conclusion, it stands to reason all Faiths can be included as all Faiths have their particular -O-image. I'm not suggesting we stop yammering about whatness, for by sharing, we get a bigger picture. I am suggesting we stop misusing our respective -O-images as clubs to beat each other up with. Each of our images is finite and no one finite is closer to The Truth than any other finite. There is one thing that can be said of -O- that is true - 'Is' and the rest are the mythos we tell each other around our respective campfires. We need to start from 'this is what -O- is like' in our theological discussions to keep us from going into Idolatry. One can understand another's stance without having to accept it and it is Mutual Understanding that can lessen strife among Believers. As far as I'm concerned, the only 'wrong' theology is the Theology of Hate, which is political rather than religious. This is where the proponents of the Single Confession make their mistake, for they assume the Confession must be about the Whatness. All they accomplish by this is to paint a picture of the sun on the window hoping nobody sees the real sun, for the real truth is "That -O- Is", not "What -O- is." It seems to me there is a fear in some circles to see that -O- is much grander than what is portrayed in the Bible, leading to accusations that different -O-images are images of different -O-s, which is no more than semantics. You talk about -O- from one perspective and I from another, but we are both talking about the same Reality. It is this Reality we have a Single Confession about.

x>x>There is one thing that can be said of -O- that is true - 'Is' and the rest are the mythos we tell each other around our respective campfires . . . One can understand another's stance without having to accept it and it is Mutual Understanding that can lessen strife among Believers.
x>I find it confusing that you talk about a truth, but you do not talk about a church.

One problem with the spontaneous nature of my mystical experiences is that I do not belong to any one school of thought. If someone wishes to learn from a Sensei, they follow the path set out before them - 'This is how I learned it. If you wish to learn it for yourself, do this and that.' You learn from those who went before and follow a map, as it were. With the traditional approach, the question is 'How do I get there?' while my question is more like 'How do I show others how to get here?'
I have come across some tricks to help smooth the way for the experience, but I cannot teach them without touching upon Zen. I cannot call myself a Zennist although others have. I cannot endorse the Zen path as that is not the one I traveled. Although I sometimes call myself a Taoist, it is more like a Taoist explanation of where I'm at without saying how I got here. While I often talk about -O- in what sounds like Hinduism, I cannot say that is the Total Truth, no matter how good it feels emotionally. There are times one must discuss -O- in the Feminine aspect, requiring one to talk of the Goddess - I suppose at those times you could call me a Celtic Taoist. Elsewhere we have discussed my respect for certain areas of Christian Philosophy. I respect much of what my Jewish friends have to say but I cannot do more than join them in the Hyphen Nation.
One of the threads I tried to start a long time ago (before Internet) was along the lines of 'what would you ask -O- if you had the right to ask one question?' If I had to chance to question Him, I would ask him why He gave me the mystical path. There are no regrets, don't get me wrong; however, it is hard to tell someone how to get here when I got teleported and have no idea how it happened. Sometimes I find it real aggravating that He would pull that kind of practical joke on me and have to fight the desire to smack Him upside the back to the head. It is real frustrating that I do not have a "Tradition" to fall back onto when attempting to talk about this stuff, for like I said in the talk about

the faith of Jesus and the Religion about Jesus, the 'Problem of Authority' is sure to raise its ugly head.

x>x> You learn from those who went before and follow a map, as it were. With the traditional approach, the question is 'How do I get there?' while my question is more like 'How do I show others how to get here?'
x>Why not draw your own map? The terrain is all the same, as you have said before. One more trail on the map will not hurt.

If I did attempt a map, it would have to be a three dimensional holographic image in order to show all the commonalities we share and it would more than likely look like a tree. The roots of the tree would represent mystical experience, the trunk representing belief in the Divine, the major branches representing various theologies, minor branches representing various schools of thought, the twigs representing various denominations, and the leaves representing the believers. One uniting factor in all Faiths is a belief in the Divine and it is from this central belief that we all branch out. Take Christianity, for example. The branch called Roman Catholicism may be a different branch on the tree of Christianity, but it is still part of the same trunk as the Southern Baptist and the Quaker. Theravada, Mahayana, and Zen Buddhists may be on different branches, but they are on the tree of Buddhism. Ultimately, each Faith is a different branch of the same tree, for the Taoist, the Hindu, and the Muslim all have faith in the Divine. As I have said many times, we all have faith in the Is part, we just differ on the What part.
Being able to draw a map depends on knowing how one got to that point. What does an eight year old know about traversing the mystical path? At the time of my initial experiences, all I knew of religion was the Presbyterian church my grandparents went to and the Baptist church my mom sent us kids to. All that was on my mind concerning matters of religion at the time was the differences in the teaching of the two churches concerning -O-'s Nature. A spot on a map indicates one has traveled a path that goes from point 'A' to point 'B', but I cannot fill in the from - to area of the map. For me, it was more like the transporter in Star Trek, one instant I was there and all the sudden I was here. I must reiterate that 'here' and 'there' are misleading terms.
This idea that using the terms 'here' and 'there' in the Spiritual sense as being equal to using them in the Physical sense is what leads people to assume a map is needed to facilitate their 'arrival' in Nirvana. It all stems from our view of the metaphysical as 'beyond', as I talked about elsewhere. Heaven, Nirvana, Moksha, Satori, or whatever you want to call it, is an internal state of mind, not some 'place' in some outer dimension. The terms 'here' and 'there', used in Spiritual language, are relative, as are 'particle' and 'wave', when used in

Quantum Mechanical language - it all depends on how you look at it in the latter and what you make of it in the former. As put in Buddhist terms, "Samsara is Nirvana"; the Sacred and the Profane are continuous territory, in other words. Rather than draw a map, I'm more interested in compiling a thesaurus. The Divine is the Divine, whether one is discussing it from a Christian or a Taoist perspective. Salvation may mean one thing to a Buddhist and something else to a Jew, but the idea of Salvation is a common concept. One thing that saddens me is the common assumption that if one does not believe in the Biblical Image, one does not believe in -O- at all. This is especially true in Christian thought, where the argument is limited to Believers against Atheists, which are but two of the many participants in the discussions at St. Pete's Bar and Grille. Not having traversed a path to get here, I can see where we all are talking about the same mountain, just from various sides.

The problem I have with maps is they imply competition, which is a wrongheaded approach as far as I'm concerned. Spirituality should be a uniter in that we believe, not a divider by what we believe. I'm not concerned that our friend over there is Jewish, this friend here is a Wiccan, that person over there is Buddhist, and so forth, what I'm concerned is in the sharing finite images of the Infinite with each other, agreeing to disagree in the details. Whatever this Reality we call -O- actually is, the terms God, G-d, Allah, Dharmakaya, Brahman, Tao, and so forth, are all equally Incomplete, for they are finite while -O- is Infinite. It is absurd to take the stance "This and only this is what God Is." The absurdity is in thinking we can limit -O- to any one daffynition, which when you think about it, is pretty disrespectful to -O- and is Idolatrous. I highly doubt -O- is concerned in how we believe, as long as we believe.

x>x>Spirituality should be a uniter in that we believe, not a divider by what we believe. I'm not concerned that our friend over there is . . . and so forth, what I'm concerned is in the sharing finite images of the Infinite with each other, agreeing to disagree in the details.
x>Are you unconcerned about the possibility there is A Truth?

There is A Truth and that is "-O- is and the rest is commentary." I freely confess that my -O-image is incomplete, after all, I'm only human, which means I comprehend in finite images while -O- is infinite, a state that cannot be imaged. Yes, there are times the Stern Father slaps you upside the back of the head for being stupid, but it is more in frustration than condemnation. There are times that -O- appears as the Loving Mother to kiss the boo-boo and make it 'all better.' as well. Sometimes there is a presence that is so awesome, it seems like blasphemy to put it to words, no matter how much you feel driven to circle the square - one might as well attempt to drink the Pacific Ocean in a single gulp.

The Hindu school of Vedanta makes for a good -O-image as does Taoist thought. The Buddhist Tathata and Sunyata both are valid -O-images as well. A thesaurus is needed as no one daffynition is 'The Truth, The Whole Truth, And Nothing But The Truth©,' when it comes to daffyfining the Infinite.

By using a thesaurus, we can walk alongside our fellow travelers for periods of time enjoying the company. An associated problem with maps is that we have a tendency to selectively ignore the landscape while we follow the map, not paying attention to the fact that the Cedar and the Pine are both trees. Buddhism and Judaism are different religions, but they are both spiritual paths. Christianity and Hinduism both have admonitions to love -O- with all ones' heart and soul. Taoism and Islam have different ideas about salvation, they just approach the issue from different angles. The Confucianist concept of Heaven is different than the Christian, but that does not mean one is True and the other False. Belief in The Divine is belief in The Divine, no matter what the cover story may be.

To be honest, I would be extremely disappointed if -O- could be reduced to A Single Truth ©. We all confess to the Infinity of -O- so how can a finite statement adequately daffyfine the Infinite? We all agree that -O- is Creator, but not all of us agree on the finer details of how it came about; is it the 'Divine Plan' of the West or the 'Surprise Me' of the East or it is something like a blend of the two? Is -O- a Being as imaged in the West, or Beingness, as imaged in the East, or some other type of critter altogether? Does -O- actually Love us, or is that the least clumsy way of talking about Divine Bliss? I know my offering of "-O- is . . . " is an attempt at a Single Truth, but I am not offering more that a confession that -O- is, not an apologetic about what in particular -O- is.

x>x>By using a thesaurus, we can walk alongside our fellow travelers for periods of time enjoying the company.

x>How does one enjoy the company of someone who has a different belief?

Realizing that no one side has a "Lock on the Truth" is paramount for all theories are equally incomplete. Think about it, -O- is much grander than our images, either singly or added. Is that not enough for celebration? It Does Not Matter that you have an image of the G-d of Judaism, she has the image of the Goddess, our friend over there the image of God, and mine is the 'one without second' of nondualistic mysticism. It Does Matter that we are each following what 'God has written on our hearts."

By sharing our visions, I feel we come closer to comprehending the Reality that is The Source of Images. One person may be partial to Italian while another may be partial to Greek food but they both can enjoy Thai without denying the other cuisines. Some wines are red while others are white; does red deny the reality of white? Some aspects of the Universe can be best explained in

Newtonian Mechanics while others are best by Quantum Mechanics; it is still the same Universe under discussion. We call light 'white', but when we spread it through a prism, a wide variety of colors emerge, with blue being just as vital as green. The continuation of the Social Order is a compromise between the Traditionalist and the Progressive forces within Society.

x>x>A thesaurus is needed as no one daffynition is 'The Truth, The Whole Truth, And Nothing But The Truth©' when it comes to daffyfining the Infinite.
x>Is not your "-O- is . . . " statement a daffynition as well?

It is merely a starting point for further discussion as the full statement is "-O- is and the rest is commentary." The closest I come to offering a daffynition is "-O- is Infinite." We have our various images of the Whatness but we all share a faith in the Isness of The Divine.
The failure to realize this concept has caused great harm to Western Spirituality as far as I'm concerned, as Western Theologians have turned an Icon into an Idol by insisting there is 'One and Only One True Image of God.' By limiting God to The Old Man on The Throne, we limit Her ability to be the Goddess, or His appearance as Krishna, or to manifest as the Tao, to mention a few images. The Old Man on The Throne is a 'what' image of God that does a disservice to the idea 'It is enough that I Am.' I submit the Western drive to formalize what this 'thatness' is makes mockery of the idea of the Infinity of The Divine. I have long found it amazing that one can consider -O- to be Infinite on the one hand while saying on the other "This and Only This is The Truth about God."
My statement is not intended to indicate that I'm calling the Old Man image 'false' as I say no more than it is an Incomplete image, much like if someone were to say that I personally, represent the entire human race. There are times I submit some people skirt the edges of Blasphemy in promoting this -O-image as The Truth For The Whole World. These people are mistaken in the idea one can equate 'Is like . . . ' with 'Is' as an Infinite can be have many aspects without becoming less Infinite. Thinking there is One True Confession confuses belief in a particular -O-image with faith in the Isness of the Source of the -O-images. It matters not so much which path we follow as that we follow a path, which is why I'm not too concerned with maps in particular, particularly one I would call 'my own.'

x>x>Thinking there is One True Confession confuses belief in a particular -O-image with faith in the Isness of the Source of the -O-images.
x>It sounds as if you're saying the image is not important.

What I'm saying is simply that an image is an image, it is not the Reality itself. Humans are just as emotionally as intellectually driven, thus we need to gnow as well as to know in order to help us come closer to comprehension. The trouble arises when we attach so much importance to the Image/Icon it takes on the status of an Idol. Your image of the Old Man on The Throne is just as important as our friend's Jewish image, this person's Islamic image, that person's Hindu image, my nonimage, and all the rest. Just as all Knowledge is equally Incomplete, all -O-images are equally Incomplete. One is no closer to The Truth no matter which image one clings to.

By elevating the Icon to Idol, we run the risk of committing Idolatry. For all my yapping about -O- as Stern Father or Caring Mother, I do not believe -O- is one or the other. I certainly am not going to be crass enough to expect you to believe the same as I do, all I ask is that you understand our differences. One can understand and disagree with a position without being disagreeable about it. For example, I agree with you that whatever it is we call -O- is the Creator of Reality. I disagree with you on Creation being an incident in the past as I submit it is a continual process. The difference is that you talk about what -O- did back then while I talk about what -O- is doing now.

I cannot condemn your position if I expect you to at least understand mine. I will not use my nonimage as a club to beat you over the head with as I hope for the same consideration from you. Once we move past "-O- is.", we misidentify the Infinite with a Finite. Yes, there are times when the only way to talk about -O- is as if He were the Old Man but there are times when one can only discuss how Mom kisses the boo boos and makes them 'all better.' Neither one, in and of itself is The Truth, just two of an infinite number of facets of the Holy Jewel that is Reality.

We do harm to the concept of -O- when we make statements along the lines of "-O- is thus and so" because if He is This, She cannot be That, which is a contradiction of the concept of Infinite. The images are important, but only up to a point. It is absurd to take an image past that point and expect it to work; One might as well drink the Pacific in one swallow or explain the Universe entirely with Newtonian Mechanics. We need the images as we communicate through imagery, but the images are like different colors in the visible bandwidth - Red does not deny Blue nor does either invalidate White. A person who cannot see the color green does not see a different world, she sees the world differently. A Name is not The Thing, A Map is not The Territory, and A Menu is not The Meal. Name, Map, and Menu are of the Mind while Thing, Territory, and Meal are of the Heart.

x>x>I freely confess that my -O-image is incomplete, after all, I'm only human, which means I comprehend in finite images while -O- is infinite, a state that cannot be imaged.

x>It sounds like you are siding with 'my words are as dirty rags'.

Not in the least. I am profoundly gratified that -O- cannot be comprehended through a particular understanding of Whatness. It Does Not Matter that my words fall short of the glory of That Which Is, it Does Matter that -O- is much grander than any and all daffynitions. To paraphrase the physicists - 'Not only is -O- grander than we imagine, -O- is grander than we can imagine.' This idea that one can reduce The Divine to a single expression has confused me for a long time. If -O- were so simple to be completely understood, it would not be -O-, would it?

I highly doubt if people realize what a degradation of the -O-concept it is to assume there is One and Only One True Image™. No matter how each of us yaps about theology, we all admit that -O- is Infinite. Whatever the Truth is, it is much more than anything that can be said or thought. For some reason, it is assumed a finite thing like language can accurately and definitely describe infinity. The most language, both that of the mind and that of the heart, can do is point to what is referenced. Where one problem arises is that we assume this pointing is outward, which comes from the assumption that Metaphysics is 'beyond' Reality, rather than being the Source of Reality. As Alan Watts put it, "God is the inside-inside of everything."

x>x> . . . not "illusion" as in fake, but "allusion", that which points to a deeper truth. x>"allusion"?

Allusion.
2: an implied or indirect reference . . .
Webesters' Divtionary

My nondualistic -O-image does not falsify your Orthodox Christian -O-image; our respective images allude to The Reality and neither is The Truth, in and of itself. Our various theologies are fingers pointing at the moon - our problem is that we mistake the finger for the moon - we compound the error by insisting others concentrate on the finger. The term "God" (Map) is not Reality (Territory) any more than the terms "Brahman", "Tao", "Heaven", "Dharmakaya", "HaShem", "Allah", or any of the ten thousand names of -O-. One can allude to the taste of a cherry pie, but the only way to be sure is to take a bite for yourself.

There is more than one way to say things, as there are many languages. The word Ki is different than Tree, but they both mean the same thing and a person can say One just as easily as Ichi. Although French is different than Greek, they both are a language as well as a cuisine. Country Western is different than Classical yet both are considered music. A picture of the Andromeda Galaxy taken under Infrared and one taken under X Ray may look different, but they are pictures of the same thing.

I know I repeat myself quite a bit on this, but this is a case where it Does Matter. To misparaphrase - there are more than two ways of looking at things. Is there really any difference between a collector of Cubist, one of Abstract, and one of Realistic art? They all collect art, just different types. By the same token, the -O-image of the Old Man, the Jewish G-d, Allah, Dharmakaya, Tao, Brahman, and Goddess, but to give name to a few are but different images of the same Reality. Each -O-image is as Incomplete as each other for an image is a Finite Construct while -O- is an Infinite Reality. A Name is nothing more than our method of talking about the thing, A Map is but a set of directions through the Territory, and A Menu is but a description of the Meal.

To semi-quote Alan Watts - one has faith in the Moon, so why rely on a picture of the Moon on the window of the mind, go outside and look. A Map implies there is only one way to traverse the Territory and many Western Maps are treated as if they were Holy Writ. A Christian Map works for a Christian, but it will not work as well for a Buddhist, and vice versa. We shouldn't expect the Map of one Faith to work for a member of another Faith; the most one can hope for is mutual understanding of our differences. In the long run, it Does Not Matter which path a person takes for in His Infinite Compassion, He is the source-end of all paths This is why I'm more concerned about a Thesaurus than a Dictionary approach to spirituality.

Spirituality is food for the soul, as I've said many times, but the trouble is that some people want to control our individual diet, as if one were supposed to eat French cuisine only. A singular diet is not only boring, it prevents one from enjoying the fatted calf of the nations. On top of that, it is hubristic; Chinese cuisine is just as tasty and good for a person. One thing we need to keep foremost in mind is 'Understanding is not condoning.' One can understand a point of view without believing it, just as one can dine on German cuisine once in a while without having it become a steady diet.

x>x>It Does Not Matter that you have an image of the G-d of Judaism, she has the image of the Goddess, our friend over there the image of God, and mine is the 'one without second' of nondualistic mysticism. It Does Matter that we are each following what 'God has written on our hearts.''

x>That is an interesting way to look at it.

I can think of no better way to celebrate the Infinity of -O- than by acknowledging "He is all things for all people." We accept the idea of different colors within 'white' light and this is no different. Some follow blue, some green, and so on. At the Source, all colors are 'white'; the individual colors are aspects of the Totality. The beauty of food is there are many methods of preparation, each as tasty as another. Like I have been saying all along, the Isness of -O- is one

---

concept we all share. Our differences are no more than green is not red and German is not Japanese. Rather than being different things, they are different aspects of the same thing.

Far too much harm has been engendered in this striving to be The One Truth, which I call the Dictionary Approach to Religion. Maps are a form of this approach in that a Christian map is different from a Buddhist map although they are both maps of the same territory. Reading from the Dictionary of Judaism leads to the 'same place' as does the Dictionary of Confucianism and there is no essential difference between retiring to a Zen or a Trappist Monastery. This is why I prefer the Thesaurus approach - mutual understanding is a better goal of Religion than mutual antagonism. The Ultimate Beauty of that which we call the Divine is available to all who seek, wherever they seek.

x>x>Our various theologies are fingers pointing at the moon - our problem is that we mistake the finger for the moon - we compound the error by insisting others concentrate on the finger.
x>How can one have a theology based on the vagueness of "Incomplete"?

The way I see it is the various theologies bring about the vagueness as theology concentrates on specific while ignoring the general. I submit that if theological discourse started with "-O- is like . . . " or "The Christian {Whatever} understanding is this . . . ", a great majority of interfaith tension would vanish. One of the leading causes of this tension is this idea that different -O-images represent "Different Gods.", extending the misunderstanding of Hindu theology onto all nontraditional theologies. Although Hindus talk about many Gods, there is only The One, the others are aspects of That Which Is. Even though a Buddhist and a Catholic will use different stories to talk about the Divine, they are still discussing the Divine. It is the stories that are different for -O- is all things to all people.

There is nothing vague about believing in a Reality that is grander than we can image, as far as I'm concerned. If One could wrap their mind around -O-, would that really be -O-? One way of looking at it is that we are all Monotheistic at the core of our belief but Polytheological in talking about it. At times, one cannot help but discuss the Stern Father and other times the Gentle Mother is the only way to talk. Sometimes one must take the approach of Tathata, at others, Sunyata. In some respects, -O- is One and in some, -O- is Many, it all depends on how one is looking at the time.

As any mystic will tell you, the Experience is far from vague for it is an experience that has all the subtlety of a sledgehammer; to semi misparaphrase Zen, it's like swallowing a red hot iron ball. With the exception of understanding, the mystical and the born again experience are the same. One expression used to talk about the Experience is 'Standing naked in the Sight of God', which can be rather unsettling. It is a humbling feeling to Know that God can See me In Every Detail, and, at the same time, it is Blissful, for I have come to realize He Loves me despite my faults. Incompleteness points out that -O- is much grander than any image we can come up with for -O- is the Source of the images. Each -O-image is Incomplete in that a -O-image points to a deeper truth rather that to itself. The idea of 'incomplete' applies not to -O- but to our understanding of Him, and is not to be taken in a derogatory context. Rather than a critique of the limitations of language, Incompleteness is a celebration that -O- is much grander than anything we can say about Him.

x>x>Far too much harm has been engendered in this striving to be The One Truth, which I call the Dictionary Approach to Religion . . . This is why I prefer the Thesaurus approach - mutual understanding is a better goal of Religion than mutual antagonism.
x>How does mutual understanding help?

It points out that we are all working for the same goal. Christian charity is promoted by one campfire story and another promotes Buddhist charity. A charitable act is a charitable act and there should be no reason a Christian and a Buddhist cannot work on the same charity. In one Faith we find "Honor thy Mother and Father" and in another we find Familial Piety with the difference being, what? Belief in -O- is belief in -O-, no matter which image one is following. Although the Christian campfire story of Salvation is different than the Hindu, they both are stories about Salvation.
As long as both are working towards the same goal, what difference does it make that they are following different paths? I admit that -O- is and you admit that God is. We both admit to the Isness and I see no reason why our -O-images must mesh in each and every detail. Your belief that God has a "Why?" for all this does not negate that I believe the reason is "Why Not?"

Dino's Daffynitionary

Dictionary Approach and Thesaurus Approach.
In the former, the definition is the reality and in the latter, the definition is an aspect of reality. Claiming the Biblical Image is the One True Image of -O- is a Dictionary approach. Claiming the Biblical Image is but one of many aspects of -O- is a Thesaurus approach.

Daffynition. {Daffyfinable, daffyfined, daffyfine, undaffyfinable, daffyscribe}
When the definition of a word or concept is treated as the reality of the concept, it becomes a daffynition - that which is taken to and or beyond a logical absurdity. For example, the sound "Whiskey" will not get a person drunk.

Incompleteness.
The concept that no matter what the field of study, there is always more to learn. In Science, for example, we can know everything about a quantity of water and the container it is in, but we cannot predict (Assuming a perfectly smooth interior) with accuracy where the first bubble will appear when we boil that water. In Theology, it is Agnostic in that a person, being finite, cannot know everything there is about -O-, but does not deny the existence of -O-.

Loyal Opposition.
The concept that one can agree with the basic premises of an idea (Such as the concept that -O- is.) but disagree with the details (Such as what -O- is.).

Meme/Memetriement
A Meme is the mental equivalent of a gene. Genes shape the physical aspects of life and memes shape the mental aspects of life. Individual Rights, Gender Roles, and Political Beliefs are examples of Memes. Mentrients are concepts that help form worldviews. The idea that a Human is a created being that is a separate reality than physical reality is a memetriement built up of memes (The arguments for the infamous Mind/Body Nonissue, for example.)

Panencarnation.
The concept that each living being is an avatar of -O-. Unlike reincarnation, there is only one soul doing all this incarnating. Panencarnation is similar to the Buddhist concept of transmigration with one exception; -O- is the one being reborn.

Panentheism.
The concept that -O- is both Totally Transcendent and Totally Immanent at the same time in the physical realm. In the mental realm, -O- is both Totally Other and Totally Self at the same time.

Rational Knowledge and Arational Gnowledge. (To Know and to Gno.)
Rational Knowledge is empirical. Arational Gnowledge is Intuitive. Neither is truer than the other and they are complimentary.

Scietheism.
Atheism based on Science.

Separation Myth.
The assumption that the two 'sides' of a dualistic equation are separate and distinct entities that can exist on their own.

Stereoscopic Consciousness.
The act of using both Rational and Intuitive modes of thought in coming to a conclusion. This is like the use of the left and the right eyes together to come up with stereo vision, which adds depth to the picture.

Symphonia Religiosa
A likening of the various Religions to the various instruments in a Symphony Orchestra. Each instrument compliments the other and although they may be playing a little differently at each moment, there is a theme to the symphony they all play to.

Theonary.
A dictionary from a particular religion.

Theosaurus.
A thesaurus of Religious terms.

LaVergne, TN USA
07 December 2010
207781LV00012B/207/P